ZION-BENTON PUBLIC LIBRARY DISTRICT

3 1126 00295 6650

Zion-Benton
Public Library District
Zion, Illinois 60099

DEMCO

AMERICAN MILITARY

INSIGNIA · MEDALS AND DECORATIONS

A M E R I C A N
M I L I T A R Y

INSIGNIA · MEDALS
AND DECORATIONS

WILLIAM FOWLER AND EVANS KERRIGAN

CHARTWELL
BOOKS, INC.

A QUINTET BOOK

Published by Chartwell Books
A Division of Book Sales, Inc.
PO Box 7100
Edison, New Jersey 08818-7100

This edition produced for sale in the U.S.A.,
its territories and dependencies only.

Copyright © 1995 Quintet Publishing Limited.
All rights reserved. No part of this publication
may be reproduced, stored in a retrieval
system or transmitted in any form or by any
means, electronic, mechanical, photocopying,
recording or otherwise, without the
permission of the copyright holder.

ISBN 0-7858-0475-7

This book was designed and produced by
Quintet Publishing Limited
6 Blundell Street
London N7 9BH

Creative Director: Peter Bridgewater
Art Director: Ian Hunt
Designers: Nicki Simmonds, Stuart Walden
Project Editors: Shaun Barrington, David Game
Editor: James McCarter
Photographer: Ian Hunt

Typeset in Great Britain by
Central Southern Typesetters, Eastbourne
Manufactured in Hong Kong by
Regent Publishing Services Limited
Printed in China by
Leefung-Asco Printers Limited

CONTENTS

SPEARHEAD

MAAG-LAOS

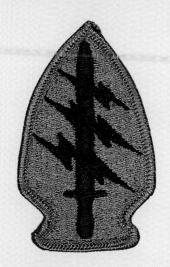

SECTION ONE

INSIGNIA

INTRODUCTION

An 82nd Airborne soldier applies camouflage to a fellow
soldier during training in the Honduras. The subdued AA
patch and airborne tab can be seen on the shoulder of
the soldier on the right of the photograph.

US soldiers stand beside their French 240mm trench mortar at Vitrey, Meurthe-et-Moselle, 21 November 1918. An officer in service dress is on the left, but most men have simple working fatigues.

The unit cloth patch on soldiers' uniforms is over 125 years old. It was born in 1862 in the American Civil War, when General Philip A. Kearney, the hard driving commander of the Federal Third Corps, assigned badges to the divisions within his corps. This was prompted, it was said, by an occasion when he mistook some officers for men of his corps and reprimanded them about their appearance. The patches worn by the Third Corps were made from cloth cut in a variety of shapes. Some of this design simplicity still exists: for example, in the red diamond patch of the 5th Infantry Division, once the patch of the 1st Division of the 5th Corps in the Civil War. The 6th and 28th Infantry Divisions in the modern US Army also retain a similar geometric simplicity. Up to World War II the 1st Corps had their original round patch and the 24th Corps a heart-shaped one.

Within a year of their introduction, Corps patches had been adopted by all the Northern armies and General Hooker had assigned colors to the divisions within each Corps. The Civil War had begun with many regiments sporting colorful uniforms, but by its close these were greatly simplified and blue and gray had become standard colors. Patches were therefore a useful way of distinguishing men and their units.

However, even today the US Army retains some of the old traditions of the 1860s, with colored piping and backings on modern dress blue uniforms. The infantry have light blue, the cavalry yellow, the artillery red, and engineers white. This light blue color appears as the backing to the Expert and Combat Infantryman's badge. The tradition is still remembered in slang — the pejorative nickname for non-airborne soldiers in the US Army is 'Legs' — an abbreviation of 'Red Legs', the term which was used for artillerymen in the Civil War because of their red or red-piped trousers.

The 'shoulder patch' as it is worn today was officially introduced into the US Army in 1918. That summer, soldiers of the 81st Infantry Division embarking at Hoboken, New Jersey, wore a hand-embroidered 'wild cat' badge on the upper left arm. When they arrived in France other US Army units adopted the idea, even though it was still unofficial. Permission to wear the insignia was given on October 19, 1918.

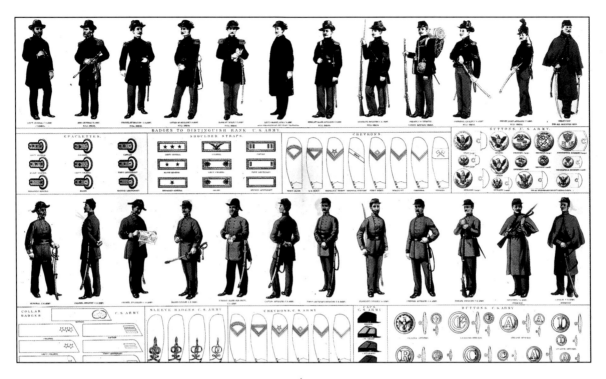

Regulation uniforms of the Civil War were more or less the same for both sides. The Confederate army was created, mostly by West Point graduates, on the same pattern as the United States army.

Though some of these badges still exist today in concept or design, many were created for the duration of World War I only and disappeared when the units were disbanded.

The Civil War origins of the unit patch reflected the problem of identifying men in a mass conscript or draft army. In time, the patch would become a focus for unit pride, which also has its reverse in ridicule for other divisional patches. The 82nd Airborne Division patch — a double 'A' for 'All American' — was read as 'Almost Airborne' by the men of the 101st Airborne. In turn the 82nd would ridicule the 'Screaming Eagle' of the 101st with references to 'Screaming Chickens'. Sometimes there was self deprecation, as when the 5th Special Forces Group in Vietnam referred to their patch as the 'Saigon Electrical Works'.

The 9th Infantry have a blue, red and white octofoil patch — the heraldic symbol of the ninth son. In Vietnam the patch was nicknamed 'Flower Power' or 'The Psychedelic Cookie' Division. In World War II men of the 90th Infantry Divison from Texas and Oklahoma asserted that the white letters 'TO', which resemble a rancher's brand, did not stand for the two states but for 'Tough Ombres' — Tough Guys. A number of the patches worn by US

Army Divisions in Europe in World War II reflected US participation in World War I: the 79th had a Cross of Lorraine and the 93rd the silhouette of a French helmet. Men of the 92nd had a Buffalo, which dated back to the Indian Wars of the Midwest, when black soldiers serving in what was traditionally a Negro division were known as 'Buffaloes' by the Indians.

After the Spanish-American War uniforms changed from blue to khaki. During World War II there was a move from khaki to olive drab and in the 1970s to camouflage colors. Throughout these transitions the principle behind unit patches remained the same. The backing material for patches and badges changed from khaki to olive drab in the 1960s. In the 1960s in Vietnam, and now privately in the United States, individual soldiers had badges embroidered directly onto their fatigue shirts and jackets.

■ CAREERS AND THE ■ 'MENU BOARD'

Rank, performance, skills or trades, length of service and unit are all displayed on different parts of a soldier's jacket or shirt. In the US Army, officers display rank on collars or epaulettes, NCOs on the upper sleeve or collar. The current unit in which a soldier is serving is worn on the left shoulder while the one in which he saw action is

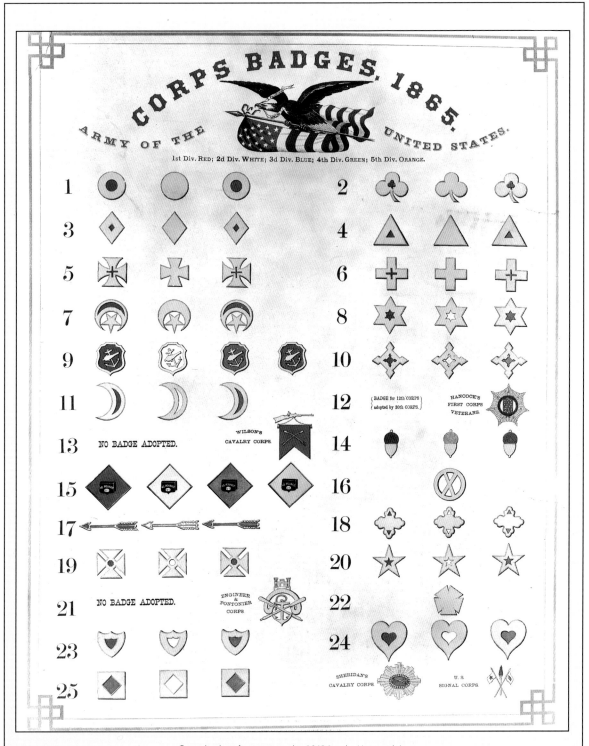

CORPS BADGES, 1865.

ARMY OF THE UNITED STATES.

1st Div. RED; 2d Div. WHITE; 3d Div. BLUE; 4th Div. GREEN; 5th Div. ORANGE.

13 — NO BADGE ADOPTED.

WILSON'S CAVALRY CORPS.

12 — { BADGE for 12th CORPS adopted by 20th CORPS. } — HANCOCK'S FIRST CORPS VETERANS.

21 — NO BADGE ADOPTED. — ENGINEER & PONTONIER CORPS.

24 — SHERIDAN'S CAVALRY CORPS. — U. S. SIGNAL CORPS.

Corps badges first appeared in 1862 (on the Union side)
and were standardized by General Hooker the following
year, who assigned colors to the divisions within each
corps.

Lieutenant General Ulysses S. Grant at Cold Harbour Virginia in June 1864. The rank insignia on the shoulders is still perpetuated in US Army Dress Blue uniforms. The business-like uniform reflects the need for comfort in the field rather than the parade ground style of peace time armies.

Reactor Operator (2nd Class NRO, 1st Class NRO and NRO Shift Supervisor). Parachutists' wings are sometimes worn informally on the front of caps and combat hats, though rank is normally displayed here. One Advisor to Vietnamese forces in the early 1960s wore an entirely non-issue black French-style beret with his wings and the distinctive floral rank badges of a captain in the Army of the Republic of Vietnam (ARVN).

In dress greens, the branch of service insignia — for example, engineers, infantry, armor or chemical corps — are displayed in gold-colored metal on a circular backing for enlisted men. They appear in other colors and without the backing for officers and are worn by all ranks on lower lapels.

Airborne wings are second only in prestige to the Ranger tab. The word 'tab' distinguishes this narrow crescent-shaped cloth badge from larger unit patches. Distinctive in black and yellow, the Ranger tab is awarded to men who have completed the gruelling training course conducted in mountain, swamp and woodland scrub terrain. A three-tour Vietnam veteran told the author that he never experienced anything as tough as Ranger training, even when he was on active operations in Vietnam.

In the 1950s the US Army introduced name tags sewn above the right pocket of shirts and jackets, while on the opposite side, in yellow letters on black, were the words 'US Army'. These distinctions made sense in a world in which many NATO and Allied armies wore very similar uniforms. The name tag was also useful for quick identification of the soldier in the field. On dress greens and other formal wear the tag is a black plastic badge with white lettering. The Vietnam War saw the move to subdued insignia and cloth name tags, and badges became a mix of black and olive drab. Patches which had been a rainbow of colors were changed to a mix of black and olive drab, though some of the texture of the black embroidery did convey an idea of the original color and design. The transition also produced some odd mixes of uniforms, with full color divisional patches contrasting with subdued name and US Army tags and even some in-country modifications.

One veteran recalled to the author how his Special Forces A and B Teams could be distinguished in base camps. The men of the A Team, who were in contact with North Vietnamese and regular VietCong forces, wore highly colored South Vietnamese and US Army insignia, including a two-color cravat. Their B Team companions, who worked in the greater security of a base supply area, had the complete subdued olive drab insignia. An uninformed visitor would have assumed from

worn on the right shoulder. Thus General Galvin, Supreme Allied Commander Europe, SACEUR, wears a 1st Cavalry patch on his right shoulder, since he served with 'the Cav' in Vietnam. Special trades or training are worn on or above shirt or jacket chest pockets. When a soldier is in dress greens with his medal ribbons, qualification and trade badges, divisional patch, rank, service stripes and name tag on his tunic he is sometimes described as wearing his 'menu board'. A knowledgable observer can read off the man's career and service simply by identifying ribbons, badges and patches.

Special skill badges include Parachutist, Senior Parachutist and Master Parachutist wings, Pathfinder, Air Assault, EOD (senior and master) Diver (in four classes) Scuba Diver and, perhaps rather chillingly, Basic Nuclear

ABOVE A meeting of minds — General Galvin SACEUR — Supreme Allied Commander Europe — receives a briefing from a CBW clad officer. General Galvin wears the 1st Cavalry patch on his right shoulder since he served with the unit in combat in Vietnam.

TOP Pvt. Willy Edward and Milton Wainsright of Co. A, 2d Bn, 30th Inf. 3 Div. on Exercise Marne Might in 1965. The Div patch can just be seen on the jacket of the right hand man.

appearances that the roles were reversed.

In part this can be explained by the fact that rear areas are where dress and insignia discipline are enforced by officers and Military Police. In the rear, troops can also retain some control over the laundering and issue of their clothing. In the field, when bundles of fatigues arrive, men rarely bother with badges and patches.

As far back as World War II badges and patches were being collected. Today, there are both fakes and forgeries on the market, as well as simply modern patches which have been made by manufacturers and never issued. Knowledgable collectors can identify fakes by the degree of wear and fading, the materials used and the quality of workmanship. However, even modern badges can be 'distressed' to look like twenty- or thirty- or even fifty-year-old insignia. New or old, the color and design of US Army patches still exert a fascination, reflecting over 100 years of history and service.

CHAPTER ONE

MAKING AND FAKING

Two officers — one a Ranger qualified soldier with the
82nd Airborne and the other a Major with the 101st with
Master Parachutist Wings discuss tactics during Exercise
Golden Pheasant in Honduras in March 1988

Over the years, US Army insignia has been produced using a variety of machine embroidery techniques. Some are very old and all have characteristic features. The first work was done in the United States in the late 1880s, on 107 class trade or Irish swing-needle machines, as they were popularly known. Domestic machines were also used and these techniques are still employed by Third World embroiderers with great skill and artistry.

From World War II to the late 1950s, the US Army wore tunics and jackets in a color generally called khaki. Correctly, it was Olive Drab Shade No 33 or No 51, and there was a lighter color Khaki, Army Shade No 1. Shoulder patches from this period have either a narrow tan or pale khaki edge, or no visible edge at all.

In 1957 the introduction of new Army Green Uniform saw the move to patches with a dark green edge. By the mid-1960s the characteristic feature of machine-made badges was the merrowed edge. This is a solid band of chain stitching which stands proud of the badge and which ends in a 'tail' of thread which is normally stuck to the back of the badge. The edge helps to protect the material and prevent fraying.

Clearly then, a World War II badge which has a merrowed edge is a modern copy. The problem with copies and fakes is where badges are produced locally by small-scale operations. During World War II the British produced equipment and clothing as well as badges for the US Army. Singer machines which could produce variable satin stitches and straight filling stitches were used. Some overseas copies of US badges are recognizable by the use of colored cloth in the construction of the badge to save thread. In early designs this was with felts, but in the Far East silks have since found favor.

Patches produced for US servicemen in Korea, Vietnam, Thailand and the Philippines have a unique charm of their own. As a rough guide, the Thai-made patches are the finest, using small panels of matched silk to make up the background colors. The least well finished are the Vietnamese-made — they were often put together on a domestic sewing machine — the problem with this is that finer detail must be done by hand. Interestingly, examples of Vietnamese badges exist in a plastic wallet with a button tag, so that they can be hung from a shirt pocket in the French style. Conventional sewing machine-made patches require the embroiderer to move the fabric so that it is oversewed many times with ordinary stitches. The Vietnamese-made patches sewn in this way are therefore rather crude. The method is unsuitable when fine detail or a heavier weight of work is required.

Philippine patches are better made and continue to be produced. One experienced American collector explained

198th Inf Brigade (subdued) – black embroidered thread on an OD cloth patch, normally the black background is also embroidered)

32nd Arty Brigade

22nd Signal Brigade (subdued, the mechanical embroidery on this patch has been incorrectly programmed and the motif is off center).

44th Medical Brigade

18th Medical Brigade

The Imjin Scouts patch on a fatigue shirt of an unnamed Spec 4 in the 2nd Infantry Division.

that he had a contact in Manilla who could make a perfect copy of any badge you could name. Valuable and rare privately-made Vietnam era badges could therefore be faked. Ageing can be achieved by an overnight soaking in coffee or a dilute soft drink and a little distressing. Stone-washed designer jeans get much the same treatment.

The Japanese and Taiwanese also produced patches and insignia during the Vietnam War and their quality is superior to any Far Eastern work. Many modern 'fun' patches are made in Taiwan.

The only way a fake patch handmade in the Far East can be identified with certainty is to examine its origins and likely availability. Where only a few hundred were produced and worn in Vietnam or Korea the chances of a real badge coming onto the market are rare.

The real problem arises with World War II, Korean or Vietnam War patches which are collectable if they are locally made. A good modern handmade copy looks like the real thing. Pakistan has an internationally-respected reputation for its gold and silver thread work — World War II badges like the China, India and Burma 'Flying Tigers' can be faked and are so collectable and attractive that they still command good prices.

The Combat Infantryman's Badge above the U.S. Army insignia over the left pocket of a fatigue shirt. The CIB with its wreath around a musket contrasts with the Expert Infantryman's Badge which is without a wreath. The CIB was awarded to men who had seen combat and variants like a Combat Medic's badge were produced for front-line support arms.

When there is no pretence at faking, many veterans are proud to wear a top-quality gold and silver thread version of their divisional patch on a blazer or jacket.

Where patches have been unstitched from a shirt or jacket the threads often remain. Though these could be faked, this is a relatively reliable and quick way of checking if the badge is authentic and has been worn on clothing. Many patches are manufactured, but never issued, and though they are good representations of insignia, they went straight from the workshop to the dealer, never stopping on a uniform en route.

Another quick check is the starch and wear on the badge. Since many have been worn on fatigue shirts the starch has entered the fabric, and they may even retain the crease from the sleeve. In addition, the effects of sunshine and rain will bleach out the color in a patch that has seen service. Locally made insignia from Vietnam are particularly prone to fading.

★

CHAPTER TWO
THE FAMILY TREE

In a classic World War II 'action' picture Doughboys
pose with infantry weapons. The man on the left with the
M1 Garand appears to have the 80th Division patch
showing the Blue Ridge Mountains on the shoulder of his
combat jacket.

US Army Engineers of the first contingent of soldiers to arrive in Glasgow, Scotland in 1917 stand with their rifles and canteens piled. The soldiers have no distinguishing features except their metal collar insignia and the cords on their campaign hats.

The structure of the US Army is rather like that of a family tree. Divided into Army units with their own area of operation and their own history and traditions, further subdivisions of Corps and Divisions follow. Each has its patch which reflects its special identity.

During World War I, some units were activated, but did not actually serve overseas. Those that did see action in France collected battle honors and insignia which reflected their service. World War II saw involvement on a larger scale and in different theaters of war. The unit patch, embroidered in silk, became a focus for pride as US Army and Air Force units mingled with Allied forces in North Africa and, toward the end of the War, in Italy and Northern Europe. In the Pacific the US Marine Corps and the US Army island-hopped toward Japan, and there was less contact with Allies. At the end of the War, some of these units were disbanded, and their patches have become collector's items. However, as the survey of Divisions below shows, many remain part of the Active Army, while others form part of the Army Reserve or the National Guard.

■ ARMY PATCHES ■

The army units are the top tier of the structure of the US armed forces. Their patches often reveal the influence of history. In the 1930s, the 1st Army's patch was an 'A' on a ground colored according to the branch of service of the wearer in the upper half of the patch. This was later simplified to a red and white ground.

The 2nd Army patch features a red and white '2' on a khaki ground. The 3rd Army has the letters 'A' and 'O', the latter commemorating the fact that it was the army of occupation in Germany in 1918. The 4th Army patch has a white four-leaf clover on red ground.

Soldiers of the 2nd Infantry Division climb the bluffs above
Omaha Beach in Normandy. The Indian Head patch is
clearly visible on their combat jackets.

The original form of the 5th Army's patch was five
stars, but this was changed to feature a silhouette of a
mosque, commemorating its organization at Oujda,
Morocco, in January 1943. The new patch was officially
approved by General Mark W. Clark.

Early versions of the 6th Army's patch were a simple
six-pointed star. Later, the letter 'A' was added. A red
triangle with seven yellow steps on either side is the
patch of the 7th Army, while the 8th Army has a white
cross on red. The 9th Army patch has an 'A' within a
petal-shaped border on a red ground.

Not shown here are the patches of the 10th Army (an
'X' formed as two triangles), and the 15th Army (an 'A'
on a five-sided shape with red and white blocks forming
a roman 'X'). The 14th Army was a 'ghost unit' which
existed on paper only.

■ CORPS PATCHES ■

As with Army patches, the Corps patches during World
War II reflect unit identity and history. A description of
each follows:

1ST CORPS

A white circle on a black field.

2ND CORPS

A 'II' flanked by the American Eagle and British Lion. 2nd
Corps landed in North Africa, and with the 4th, 6th and
21st subsequently fought in Italy.

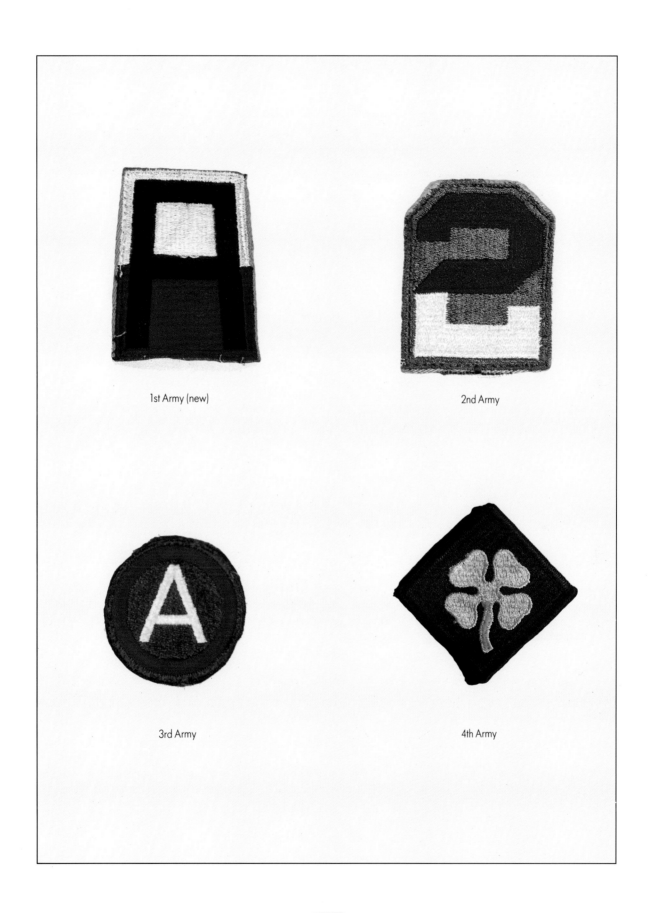

1st Army (new)

2nd Army

3rd Army

4th Army

5th Army (new)

6th Army

7th Army

8th Army

OD service jacket used by a medical corps Sergeant on demobilization after World War II. The meritorious service insignia is displayed on the right forearm and the discharge insignia is above the right breast pocket.

General Mark W Clark in an open air HQ in Italy. The 5th Army patch is just visible on his shoulder and his general's stars on shirt collar and overseas cap. The WAC with the telephone has the chevrons of a Technician 4th Grade.

3RD CORPS

A caltrop insignia in blue with black border (a caltrop is a spiked device used to hobble horses or pierce pneumatic tires). 3rd Corps is nicknamed 'Phantom Corps' following its surprise attacks on German forces in the Ardennes in 1944-45. Today, 3rd Corps is the Reforger force for rapid reinforcement of NATO in Europe.

4TH CORPS

A circle divided in four blue and white segments.

5TH CORPS

A five-sided blue patch with white edges.

6TH CORPS

A '6' on a blue circle.

7TH CORPS

Originally a '7' on a six-pointed shield, but this was changed to a 'VII' on a red seven-pointed star.

8TH CORPS

An '8' on a blue field.

9TH CORPS

A red 'IX' on a blue field.

10TH CORPS

A 'X' on a blue and white field.

11TH CORPS

Originally a heraldic shield, changed to two dice showing the score of 11.

12TH CORPS

A windmill representing New Amsterdam (New York).

13TH CORPS

To avoid the unlucky associations of the number, a green four-leaf clover and red triangle was adopted.

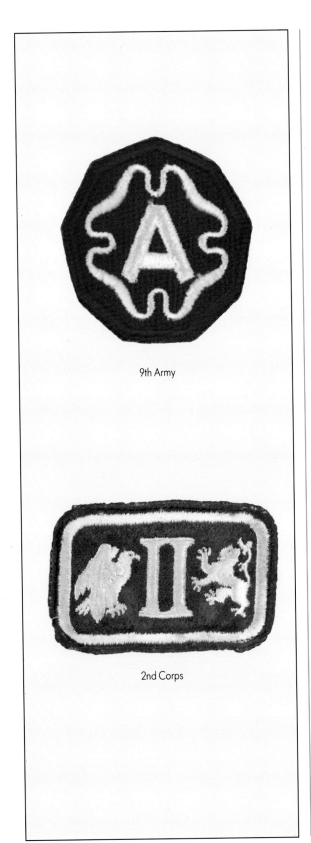

9th Army

2nd Corps

Radio operators of Co B, 503rd Inf Battle Group, 82nd Airborne Division during a live firing exercise 'Sunshade IV' at Fort Bragg in January 1963. They have full color insignia and characteristic airborne boots and pants.

14TH CORPS
A blue 'X' and a red four-pointed star.

15TH CORPS
Originally a blue and white 'XV', but this was changed to a more original design with the 'X' superimposed upon the 'V'.

16TH CORPS
A shield with a blue border enclosing a four pointed star. The star is surrounded by a white serrated circle.

17TH CORPS
Interestingly there is no evidence of a patch for the 17th Corps. It does not even appear to have been a 'ghost' unit.

18TH CORPS
Originally a blue dragon's head set at an angle on a diamond-shaped field. When the 18th became an Airborne corps, the Airborne tab was placed square above, with the dragon looking down to the left.

19TH CORPS
Originally the Liberty Bell in red with yellow border. This was changed to a white tomahawk on a blue, white-bordered circle.

20TH CORPS
Two yellow interlocked 'X's on a shield.

ZION-BENTON PUBLIC LIBRARY DISTRICT

3rd Corps

5th Corps

8th Corps

10th Corps

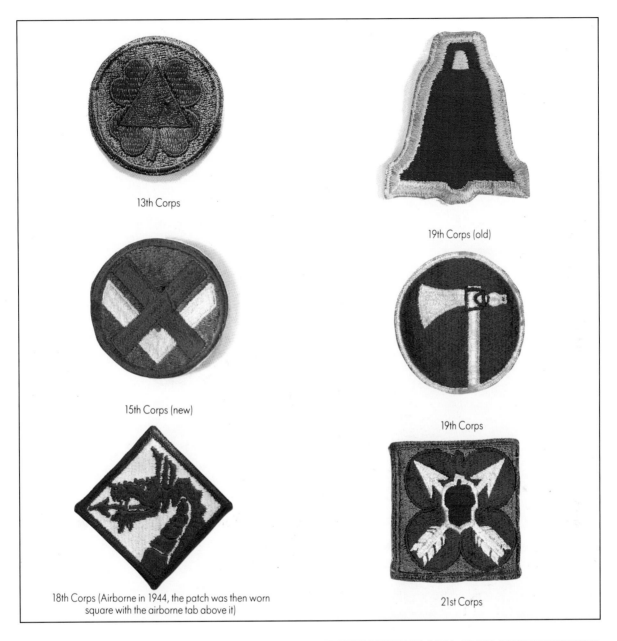

13th Corps

19th Corps (old)

15th Corps (new)

19th Corps

18th Corps (Airborne in 1944, the patch was then worn square with the airborne tab above it)

21st Corps

OPPOSITE Anonymous in British snow camouflage overalls a 81mm mortar M1 crew prepare to fire on a German position near St Vith, Belgium, 1944.

21ST CORPS
A red acorn pierced by two arrows.

22ND CORPS
An arrowhead.

23RD CORPS
Three crossed arrows.

24TH CORPS
A heart, the insignia first adopted by the 24th during the Civil War.

36TH CORPS
A blue patch with an interlocked '3' and '6', plus a red and white three-pointed star interlocked with a smaller star.

The 31st and 33rd Corps were 'ghost units', which existed on paper only during World War II.

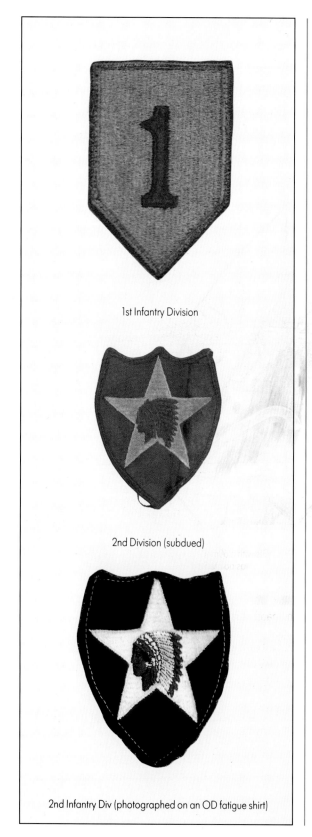

1st Infantry Division

2nd Division (subdued)

2nd Infantry Div (photographed on an OD fatigue shirt)

■ DIVISIONAL PATCHES ■

Divisonal patches are perhaps the best known of all the insignia in the US Army. Being smaller units, the divisions became the focus of the serving soldier's loyalty and pride, and many divisions have nicknames and mottoes, giving them a particular individual identity. The divisional patches were worn in both World Wars, and many divisions also saw service in Korea and in Vietnam during the post-World War II period. A brief description of each Division's insignia and history is given below:

1ST INFANTRY DIVISION

'The Big Red One', originally formed as the First Expeditionary Division in World War I. In World War II it fought Rommel's Afrika Corps in North Africa, and was also operational in Sicily. It landed at Omaha Beach and advanced with the Allies into Germany. 1st Inf. Div. served a total of 1,656 days in Vietnam. It is an Active Army Division based at Fort Riley, Kansas, and at Goppingen, West Germany.

2ND INF. DIV.

With its 'Indian Head' patch, 2nd Inf. Div. saw action in both World Wars. In World War II it fought in Normandy, the Ardennes and in Czechoslovakia, and later saw action in Korea. It is an Active Army Division, based at Camp Casey, Republic of South Korea.

3RD INF. DIV.

The 'Marne', an honor earned during their service in World War I. The patch is three white bars on a blue background, which is the Infantry color. The narrow border is all that remains of an original Khaki ground. In World War II, the Marne saw action in Sicily, Cassino, Anzio, the Colmar Pocket and Munich. It also served in the Korean War. An Active Army Division, it is based at Wurzburg, West Germany.

4TH INF. DIV.

The 'Ivy Division', with a khaki diamond-shaped patch containing a green four-pronged, four-leafed ivy. Originally, the patch was tombstone-shaped. The 4th fought in France in both World Wars, and was the first US Division to enter Paris in 1944, and later, to reach German soil. It served a total of 1,534 days in Vietnam and is based at Fort Carson, Colorado.

5TH INF. DIV.

The 'Red Diamond' Division fought in both World Wars, and its 1st Brigade served in Vietnam between 1968 and

1971. It is Active Army Division with Reserve elements, based at Fort Polk, Louisiana.

GIs with a 60mm mortar M2 in World War II. The censor has painted out the insignia on their helmets.

6TH INF. DIV.

During World War I the 6th 'Sight-seeing' Inf. Div. patch was a small red six-pointed star with a '6' in center. The number has since gone and the star grown larger. The 6th served in New Guinea and the Philippines in World War II. It is an Active Army Division with Reserve and National Guard elements, based at Fort Richardson, Arkansas.

7TH INF. DIV.

The 'Hourglass' patch is formed by two crossed '7's, one of which is inverted. The 7th served in both World Wars and also in Korea. It is an Active Army Division, based at Fort Ord, California.

8TH INF. DIV.

The patch has an '8' pierced by a Golden Arrow. It served in both World Wars and received its nickname of 'Pathfinder Division' serving in Brittany, Duren and Cologne during World War II. An Active Army Division, it is based at Bad Kreuznach, West Germany.

9th INF. DIV.

The 'Old Reliables', or 'Varsity' were constituted on August 1, 1940, at Fort Bragg, and subsequently served in North Africa, Sicily, the Cotentin Peninsula and Germany. 3rd Brigade was part of the Riverine Force in Vietnam and served 985 days. Its insignia is a nine-petaled flower in red and blue. The 9th is an Active Division, with National Guard elements, based at Fort Lewis.

Paratroops of the 101st struggle with a crashed glider after landings in Holland in September 1944. The censor has scratched out the Screaming Eagle patch on the combat jackets and helmets, but their Stars and Stripes arm bands and patches are clearly visible.

10TH INF. DIV.

In World War I, the patch was an 'X' within a circle. During World War II, the Division trained for mountain operations and adopted crossed bayonets, and had the tab 'Mountain' above, which earned the nickname of 'Mountaineers'. It served on the Gothic Line and the Po Valley. An Active Division with National Guard elements, it is based at Fort Drum, New York State.

11TH INF. DIV.

11th became an Airborne Division in World War II, and adopted a new patch with Airborne tab and a winged '11' inside a shield, and gained the nickname 'Angels'. In World War II, the 11th served at Leyte, Manilla and Cavite.

12TH INF. DIV.

In World War I, the 12th had a diamond-shaped patch containing a bayonet, two stars and the figure '12'. By World War II this had changed to a yellow steer's head on a red shield. Action in the Pacific earned the nickname of 'Philippine'.

13TH INF. DIV.

The 13th's World War I insignia featured a '13' within a lucky horseshoe and a black cat. On becoming Airborne in World War II it adopted a winged unicorn inside a shield and Airborne tab. The Division served in Europe.

14TH INF. DIV.

Formed in World War I and called the Wolverine Division, the patch featured a silhouette of a wolverine within a shield.

17TH INF. DIV.

'Thunder from Heaven'. The patch features an eagle's claw within a circle and an Airborne tab. The Division participated in the Rhine crossings in 1945.

18TH INF. DIV.

'Cactus' Division — the patch features an '18' within a

3rd Infantry Div

4th Infantry Div

5th Infantry Div

6th Infantry Div

7th Infantry Div

8th Infantry Div

8th Inf Div (subdued)
Actual size same as 23rd Div bottom right

9th Infantry Div

10th Infantry Div (trained for mountain warfare, the
Division later wore a Mountain tab above its patch)

11th Airborne Div

17th Airborne Div

23rd (Americal) Div

Men of the 4th Infantry Division shelter behind the sea wall at Utah beach during the landings at Normandy in June 1944. The censor has obscured the patches for security reasons, but the diamond shape is just visible.

clump of cacti and the motto: *Noli Me Tangere* (Do not touch me). The Division was formed in World War I.

19TH INF. DIV.

Another World War I formation. The patch shows a 'G' within a circle and inverted triangle.

23RD INF. DIV.

The 'American'. Its patch shows the stars of the Southern Cross on a blue shield. In World War II, the American served in Guadalcanal, Bougainville and Cebu Island, and became part of the occupation force in Japan. In Vietnam, it was described as: 'the Army's only named Division on active service'.

24TH INF. DIV.

The 'Victory' Division's patch shows a green taro leaf (a common tropical plant) against a red circle. In World War II it saw action in New Guinea and the Philippines, and later fought in Korea. An Active Army Division, with National Guard elements, it is based at Fort Stewart, California.

25TH INF. DIV.

A red taro leaf with a bolt of lightning — hence its name, 'Tropic Lightning'. The Division was formed in Hawaii in 1941 and was at Pearl Harbor when the Japanese attacked. Later in World War II it served in Guadalcanal, New Georgia and the Philippines. It also saw action during the Korean and Vietnam Wars. An Active Army Division, the 25th is based at Schofield Barracks, Hawaii.

26TH INF. DIV.

The 'Yankees'. Their patch has the letters 'Y' and 'D' as a monogram cattle-brand on a khaki diamond. It served in Europe in World War I and fought in the Battle of the Bulge in World War II. It is now part of the National Guard and is based at Boston, Massachusetts.

27TH INF. DIV.

The 'New York' has a brand-style monogram 'NY' in red

24th Infantry Div

25th Infantry Div (Vietnamese made pocket insignia)

on a black field. In World War I it incorporated the constellation of Orion on its patch as a pun on its commander's name — Maj. Gen. J. F. O'Ryan. During World War II, the 27th fought in the Makin Islands, Saipan and Okinawa.

28TH INF. DIV.

The 'Keystone' is the red keystone of the State Seal of Pennsylvania, and had the alternative name of 'the bucket of blood'. As well as service during World War I, the 29th was in on the liberation of Paris and the fighting in Hurtgen Forest and the Colmar Pocket in World War II. It is now part of the National Guard, and is based at Harrisburg, Pennsylvania.

29TH INF. DIV.

The 29th incorporated the blue and gray colors of the two sides in the Civil War into a Ying-Yang symbol. It fought in both World Wars and is now part of the National Guard, based at Fort Belvoir, Virginia.

30TH INF. DIV.

'Old Hickory' — a patch with 'XXX' within an 'H', which is in turn encompassed by the letter 'O'. The 30th saw service in World War I and fought at St Lo, Aachen, Malmedy, Stavelot and in the Rhine crossings in World War II.

31ST INF. DIV.

The 'Dixie Division' has two back-to-back 'D's on its patch. It fought in World War I and in the Philippines in World War II.

32ND INF. DIV.

The 'Red Arrow' originally had its red arrow with a bar on a khaki ground, but this was later removed to produce an austere Divisional patch. Active in World War I, the 32nd also fought in the Pacific in World War II.

33RD INF. DIV.

Known as the 'Prairie', the patch is a yellow cross against a black circle. The Division fought in World War I and in northern Luzon, in the Philippines, in World War II.

34TH INF. DIV.

Nicknamed the 'Red Bull', the 34th had the motto 'Sandstorm Division' in World War I, and the patch had a red bull's skull and the number '34'. In World War II this had been simplified to the skull on a black background shaped like the Mexican *olla*, or flask. The Division fought in Tunisia, Cassino, the Gothic Line and the Po Valley.

35TH INF. DIV.

The 'Santa Fe' adopted the cross symbol used to mark the Santa Fe trail. It fought in Europe in both World Wars and is currently part of the National Guard, based at Fort Leavenworth, Kansas.

36TH INF. DIV.

The 'Texas' patch has a khaki 'T' inside a blue-gray shape resembling a flint arrowhead. The 36th fought in World War I and at Salerno, Cassino and in France and Germany during World War II.

37TH INF. DIV.

An Ohio Division with a patch of a red circle within a white border, earning the nickname of 'Buckeye'. It fought in World War I and at Munda, Bougainville, Lingayen Gulf and Manilla in World War II.

38TH INF. DIV.

Known as 'Cyclone Division'. The patch has the letters 'C' and 'Y' within a blue and red shield. It fought in World War I and at Bataan in World War II.

39TH INF. DIV.

'Delta Division' fought in World War I, but did not go overseas in World War II. Its original patch was a circle with a triangle enclosing three smaller triangles in red, white and blue, symbolizing the three states of the Mississsipi delta: Mississipi, Louisiana and Arkansas. The patch was simplified to a red triangle enclosing the letter 'D'.

40TH INF. DIV.

The 'Sunburst Division' — its patch has a gold sun on a blue diamond. It fought in both World Wars and in Korea. It is currently part of the US Army Reserve and National Guard, based at Los Alamitos, California.

41ST INF. DIV.

'Sunset' or the 'Jungleers' — a semi-circular patch showing a Pacific Ocean sunset. The Division fought in World War I and at Salamaua, the Marshall Islands, Mindanao and Palawan in World War II.

42ND INF. DIV.

The 42nd 'Rainbow' Division fought in World War I and at Schweinfurt and Munich in World War II, when it also liberated Dachau.

43RD INF. DIV.

Known as 'Red Wing', or 'Winged Victory', the 43rd has

25th Infantry Div

26th Infantry Div

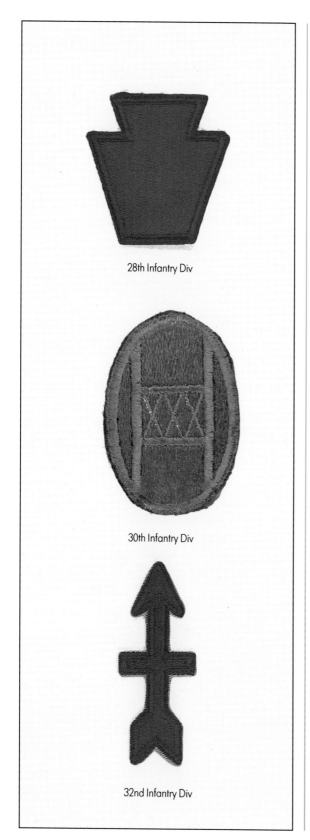

28th Infantry Div

30th Infantry Div

32nd Infantry Div

a patch with a black grape leaf on a red background, symbolizing the four states of New England. The 43rd fought in New Georgia, New Guinea and Luzon in World War II.

44TH INF. DIV.
The patch has two blue figure '4's back-to-back, forming an arrowhead on a yellow background. It served in the Saar, Ulm and Danube rivers during World War II.

45TH INF. DIV.
A yellow Indian thunderbird on a red diamond gives the unit its nickname. An earlier patch had a yellow swastika — insignia hardly suitable during World War II, where it saw action at Salerno, Cassino and the Belfort Gap. It also served in Korea. The patch is still worn by the 45th Infantry Brigade (Separate) of the Oklahoma Army National Guard, which replaced the Division in 1968.

46TH INF. DIV.
Although assigned two patches, this was a 'ghost unit' in World War II.

47TH INF. DIV.
The patch features a Viking helmet — the Division was reputed to have a large number of Norwegian Americans. It is part of the National Guard, based at St Paul, Minnesota.

48TH INF. DIV.
Another 'ghost' division.

49TH INF. DIV.
The patch features a gold-panner on a red and yellow shield.

50TH INF. DIV.
A 'ghost' division.

51ST INF. DIV.
A yellow and blue five-sided patch with a rattlesnake motif.

55TH INF. DIV.
A 'ghost' division.

59TH INF. DIV.
A 'ghost' division.

63RD INF. DIV.
'Blood and Fire' — the 63rd has a red, drop-shaped

33rd Infantry Div

34th Infantry Div

39th Infantry Div

40th Infantry Div

41st Infantry Div

46th Division

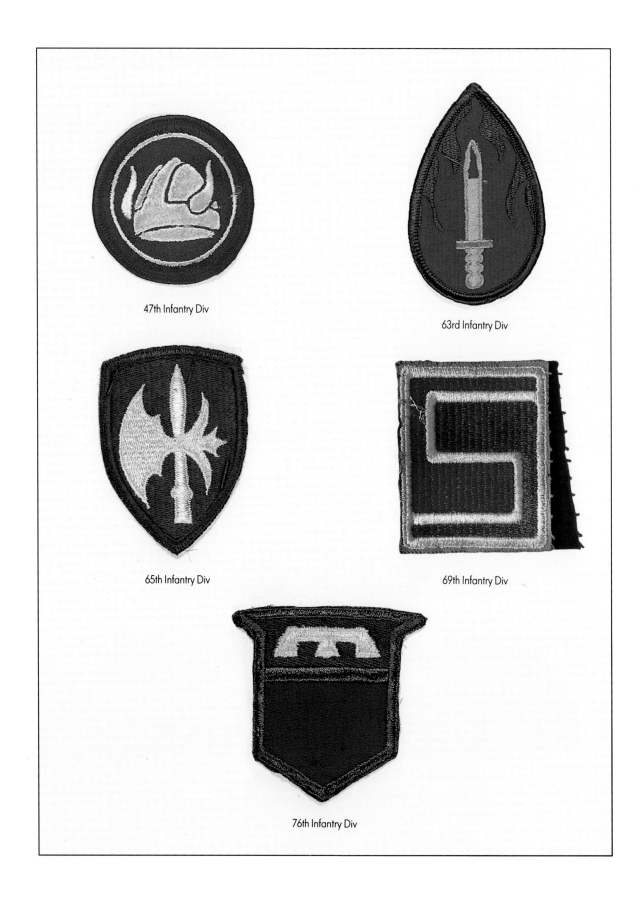

47th Infantry Div

63rd Infantry Div

65th Infantry Div

69th Infantry Div

76th Infantry Div

patch terminating in fire, enclosing a yellow bayonet with a drop of blood on the tip. It fought in Bavaria and on the Danube during World War II.

65TH INF. DIV.
The patch features a white halberd within a blue shield — hence the name 'Battle-Axe'. It fought in Saarlautern, Regensburg and on the Danube during World War II.

66TH INF. DIV.
During World War I, the 66th had a circular patch showing a black panther. In World War II this was changed to a snarling panther's head. It may have been thought that the first patch looked too much like a domestic cat, or that it was too similar to the patch of the 81st Division (see illustration on page 38). The 66th bottled up German forces at St Nazaire and Lorient during World War II.

69TH INF. DIV.
The 'Fighting Sixty-Ninth' has the figures '6' and '9' interlocked in blue and red. It saw action in Germany during World War II.

70TH INF. DIV.
The 'Trailblazers' have a rather quaint patch showing a white woodsman's axe with a green tree and white mountain in the background, all on a red field. The Division served at Saarbrucken and on the Moselle River during World War II.

71ST INF. DIV.
'The Red Circle' — a circular white patch, bordered in red, containing the figures '7' and '1' set at an angle. The 71st served in southern Germany in World War II.

75TH INF. DIV.
The 75th's patch has a '7' and '5' against a red, white and blue shield. The Division served in the Ardennes and Westphalia in World War II.

76TH INF. DIV.
The 'Liberty Bell' — the shield-shaped patch is red in the lower half and blue at the top with white motif. It saw action in World War I and in Luxembourg and Germany in World War II.

77TH INF. DIV.
The Division of New York State, the 'Statue of Liberty' patch has the statue in yellow outline. It fought in World War I and in Guam, Leyte and Okinawa in World War II.

GIs on the way to Normandy wear a khaki sleeve over their Divisional Patches. This simple security precaution would prevent identification of the unit when it embarked or disembarked and would save the censor the task of erasing the insignia from photographs.

78TH INF. DIV.
The 'Lightning' Division — the patch features a white lightning bolt on a red semi-circle. It fought in World War I and at Aachen and the Roer and Ruhr rivers in World War II.

79TH INF. DIV.
'Lorraine' — a white Cross of Lorraine on a blue shield. The patch commemorates the Division's service in France in World War I. It returned to France in World War II, seeing action in the Vosges and in Normandy.

80TH INF. DIV.
The 'Blue Ridge' Division's patch in World War I showed blue ridges with the motto: 'Vis Montium', and the figure '80'. In World War II, when the Division fought in Normandy, the Moselle and at the Relief of Bastogne, the patch was simplified to show just three ridges, representing the three States of Pennsylvania, Virginia and West Virginia.

77th Infantry Div

81st Infantry Div

81ST INF. DIV.

The 'Wild Cat' — the patch shows a black, stub-tailed cat against a khaki background. The Division fought in World War I and at Angaur, Peleliu and Ulithi in World War II.

82ND INF. DIV.

The 'All American' Division added its Airborne tab in World War II, where it fought in Sicily, Normandy and the Ardennes. It earned the nickname 'Baggypants' after a German officer had described 82nd Division paratroopers as 'devils in baggy pants'. Its 3rd Brigade saw service in Vietnam, and it is currently an Active Army unit based at Fort Bragg, North Carolina.

83RD INF. DIV.

The 'Ohio' or 'Thunderbolt' Division. The patch has a yellow monogram reading 'OHIO' on a black triangle. The Division fought in World War I and in Italy and Germany in World War II.

84TH INF. DIV.

In World War I, the 'Railsplitters' had a circular patch with an axe head and the number '84' surmounted with the name of 'Lincoln'. In World War II — where they fought in Ardennes and at Hanover — the patch was simplified to a white axe splitting a rail.

85TH INF. DIV.

The 'Custer Division' patch had the letters 'C' and 'D' in red on a khaki circle. The 85th fought in World War I and in Italy in World War II.

86TH INF. DIV.

The 'Black Hawk' Division patch has a red shield with a black hawk, with a smaller shield bearing the letters 'BH'. It saw service in World War I and fought in southern Germany and liberated Dachau in World War II.

87TH INF. DIV.

The patch has a yellow acorn on a green circle — hence the name 'Golden Acorn'. The Division served in both World Wars, seeing action in the Ardennes, Germany and on the Czech border in World War II.

88TH INF. DIV.

Known as the 'Cloverleaf', the patch features two figure '8's combined to make a clover-leaf shape. However, the Division preferred to adopt the name 'Blue Devil'. In World War II it saw action in northern Italy.

89TH INF. DIV.

The patch has an 'M' within a circle which, when inverted becomes a 'W' — hence the name 'Rolling W', standing for Middle West. It fought in World War I and at Bingen, Eisenach and central Germany in World War II.

82nd Airborne Div

86th Infantry Div

90th Infantry Div

82nd Airborne Div (subdued)

88th Infantry Div

94th Infantry Div

95th Infantry Div

90TH INF. DIV.

The 'Tough Ombres' mentioned in the introduction. The 90th fought in World War I and saw action in Normandy, Metz and Czechoslovakia in World War II.

91ST INF. DIV.

The 'Wild West' patch features a green fir tree. The Division fought in both World Wars, seeing action in Italy during World War II.

92ND INF. DIV.

The 'Buffaloes' — a black buffalo on a khaki patch dates back to the Indian Wars of the last century. They served in both World Wars.

93RD INF. DIV.

The 93rd's patch reflects their service in World War I, when they were assigned to the French Army. It features a French World War I helmet in green on a black ground. The 93rd saw action in the Pacific in World War II.

94TH INF. DIV.

The earlier 94th patch showed a New Englander with a blunderbus on his shoulder. This was changed to a more prosaic circular patch with '9' and '4' in khaki and black during World War II, when the Division served in Brittany, the Siegrfried Line, the Saar and the Moselle River.

95TH INF. DIV.

Originally, the patch showed a K-shaped design within an oval. This was replaced by a red '9' with a white 'V' interlaced within an oval. The 'Victory' Division served at Metz, the Moselle River, the Siegfried Line and the Saar during World War II.

96th INF. DIV.

The 'Deadeye' Division had interlocked white and blue diamonds on a khaki background. It served in the Pacific during World War II.

97TH INF. DIV.

The patch was a white trident on a blue shield, hence the name 'Trident'. It served in central Germany in World War II.

98TH INF. DIV.

The 'Iroquois' patch was a shield in the colors of New Amsterdam with the head of an Iroquois indian in the center. It saw action in the Pacific during World War II.

99TH INF. DIV.

The patch is a black shield with a blue and white checkered band. The 'Checkerboard' served in the Ardennes and was at the Remagen bridgehead during World War II.

100TH INF. DIV.

The 'Century' patch has the number '100' in white and yellow on a blue shield. It served at Bitche, the Remagen bridgehead and the Saar during World War II.

101ST INF. DIV.

The 'Screaming Eagle' is, in fact, Old Abe, the mascot of the Iron Brigade in the American Civil War — the black shield of the patch also commemorates the Iron Brigade. The Division became Airborne in 1943, and served in Normandy and at Bastogne. The Division was committed to Vietnam in 1967 and served a total of 1,573 days. When subdued olive drab and black insignia were introduced in Vietnam, the Division, proud of its Screaming Eagle, retained the patch in full color. It is now an Active Airmobile helicopter-borne Division, based at Fort Cambell, Kentucky, and Fort Rucker, Alabama.

102ND INF. DIV.

The patch has the letter 'O' circling a 'Z', standing for the Ozark Mountains. The Division served on the Siegfried line and at the Ruhr and Munchen-Gladbach in World War II.

103RD INF. DIV.

The 'Cactus' Division. The patch shows a green cactus against a yellow circle. It served at Stuttgart and in Austria in World War II.

104TH INF. DIV.

The 'Timber Wolf' — the patch features a gray timber wolf's head against a green circle. The Division was prominent during the Rhine crossing at Cologne and the Ruhr in World War II.

106TH INF. DIV.

The 'Golden Lion' — a lion's head on a blue circle edged with white and red. The Division served at St Vith and in the Ardennes during World War II.

96th Infantry Div

101st Airborne Div

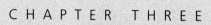

CHAPTER THREE

OTHER PATCHES:
CAVALRY, ARMORED DIVISION
AND BRIGADE PATCHES

A UH-1B Huey of the 1st Cavalry (Air Cav) lifts off from a
jungle LZ during operations in South Vietnam. The 1st
Cavalry were a pioneer force in airmobile operations
during the Vietnam War.

The patches of US Cavalry preserve the traditional yellow which first appeared in bandanas and piping on uniforms.

The 1st Cavalry — the 'First Team' or 'Hell for Leather' — saw action in the Philippines and was the first division to enter Tokyo. It served in Korea and was the first unit to enter Pyongyang in 1950. In Vietnam, it became an Air-mobile division and was credited with 2,056 days overseas and participated in many of the major operations.

It was reorganized into an armored division in 1975 and is currently an Active Army and Army National Guard Division, based at Fort Hood, Texas.

The 2nd Cavalry Division, like the 3rd, 21st, 24th, 56th, 61st, 62nd, 63rd, 64th, 65th and 66th, did not see action in World War II.

The 2nd and 3rd Cav., like 1st Cav., have yellow shield patches measuring 14×10 cm. The patches were said to have been designed by an officer's wife at Fort Bliss to be big enough to be visible through the dust kicked up by horse-mounted cavalry.

A young trooper of 1st Cavalry on Certain Strike in 1987. The patch on battle dress utilities is no longer the striking yellow shield that could be seen in the dust from mounted cavalry, but rather a subdued green and black.

The 1st Cavalry's yellow shield has an oblique black bar and outline of a horse's head. The 2nd Cav.'s patch has a blue chevron and two stars, while 3rd Cav. have one with the figure '3' in blue. The 21st and 24th Cav. have the outline of a stirrup, while the 56th have a star. The 61st has a horse's head within a spur on a yellow shield, the 62nd a shield with crossed yellow bars and the 63rd a yellow square with crossed red bars. The 64th Cav.'s patch shows a saber on a yellow field, and the 65th's an arrowhead on a blue and yellow shield. The 66th has a six-pointed yellow star with a blue border.

■ BRIGADE PATCHES ■

A common, but not universal feature of US Army Brigade patches is the four-sided shape with a slight convex bulge at the top and bottom. For many National Guard

Armored Forces Headquarters

1st Armored Div

2nd Armored Div

Brigades there is a strong State loyalty, and so the introduction of patches which reflected this was important for morale — particularly in the social climate of the 1960s.

Exceptions to the four-sided Brigade patches include shields, diamonds and circles. Some National Guard and Active Army Brigades were authorized in the 1960s to wear the World War II Divisional patch which corresponds to their number, thus perpetuating the memory of several famous Divisions. Examples of this include the 32nd Inf. Brigade which has the red arrow of the 32nd Infantry Div., the 33rd Inf. Brigade which has the yellow cross on a black circle of the 38th Inf. Div., the 40th Inf. Brigade with the gold sun on a blue diamond of the 40th Inf. Div., the 45th Inf. Brigade which has the Thunderbird of the 45th Inf. Div., though the 71st Airborne Bde., which is part of the Texas National Guard, has the insignia of the 36th Inf. Div.

Arm colors distinguish many brigade patches. So, for example, infantry have a predominantly blue design; artillery, red; medical, purple and military police, green. Artillery Brigades have arrows, cannon and missiles in yellow on a red field. Signals have lightning bolts, while logistics and transportation brigades have variations on yellow wheels against a brown field. Engineer units favor the castle of the Corps of Engineers and Civil Affairs have variants of a sword and pen or the torch of learning on blue.

One observer has noted the mixed heraldic origins of US Army Divisional and Brigade patches. Some draw on German and European designs and others on the shapes of native American patchworking traditions from the 19th century. Others, like the 81st Inf. Brigade, use designs borrowed from Red Indian totem poles. Some Hawaiian National Guard units have designs which look similar to the Japanese clan *mon*. The mon was a crest worn on uniform and equipment in the great civil wars of the 16th century. The list that follows is not complete, but rather an attempt to show the origins and designs of some Brigade patches.

The 1st and 2nd Inf. Brigades were part of 1st Inf. Div. in World War II, but were reorganized as Airborne Brigades in summer 1943. Disbanded at the end of the War, they were reactivated as independent Infantry Brigades in 1958 and returned to 1st Inf. in 1962.

1st Inf. Bde. has a white '1' on a blue background, 2nd has a blue and a white bayonet.

Post-war Germany—Pvt, 1st Class Melin Leimons of Co. C, 1st Bn. 16th Inf. Bde. of the 1st Infantry Div. shows the working parts of an M60 to Hugo Keindengon.

2nd Armored Div (subdued)

3rd Armored Div

4th Armored Div

8th Armored Div

10th Armored Div

49th Armored Div

An M113 of M troop, 3rd Squadron, 11th Armored
Cavalry Regt covers a hedge line ten miles south west of
Ben Cat, South Vietnam.

High technology logistics — a soldier of the 13th (US)
Support Command checks off vehicles with a light pen
and a bar-coded inventory.

11th Inf. Bde. has three arrows which resemble the figure '11' and also an arrow marking a breakthrough on a map. The insignia was approved on July 1966.

29th Inf. Bde., which is part of the Hawaiian National Guard, had a patch which resembled an aiming mark or sight, but this was replaced by a blue cross. The new insignia was approved in 1968.

36th Inf. Bde. is part of the Texas National Guard and so has a lone star on a blue shield.

39th Inf. Bde., part of the Arkansas National Guard, adopted a patch in 1968 which featured a white Bowie knife on a blue and red field.

40th Armored Bde., part of the California National Guard, has the sun-burst insignia of the 40th Inf. Div., but also two lightning bolts on a blue and red field.

41st Inf. Bde. has two crossed barbed arrows or harpoons on a blue and white field. The insignia was approved in June 1969.

49th Inf. Bde. is part of the California National Guard and has a cactus rose on a yellow and blue shield with a yellow diamond.

49th Armd. Bde. is part of the Texas National Guard and has the lone star and yellow, red and blue triangle of the US Armored Corps.

The 53rd Inf. Bde., part of the Florida National Guard, was formed as an armored unit in December 1964 and became an Infantry Brigade in 1968. It has a Spanish conquistador's helmet as part of the patch, but retains the tricolored Armored Corps design.

67th Inf. Bde., part of the Nebraska National Guard, has a patch approved in June 1964, featuring a pike on a blue field.

69th Inf. Bde., Kansas National Guard. The patch was approved in December 1964 and resembles a flower in a water course.

72nd Inf. Bde., Texas National Guard, had their insignia in the colors of the State flag approved in 1968.

81st Inf. Bde., Washington National Guard, has the Indian symbol of the raven. The patch was approved in May 1970.

86th Armd. Bde. has a stag's head on the red, yellow and blue of the Armored Corps.

Men of 5th Armored Div, 46th Armd Inf. Bn. in their White halftrack named Copenhagen pass a burning building. The vehicle is loaded with stores, ammunition and captured items.

171st Inf. Bde. and 172nd Inf. Bde. are Alaskan units and both have a bayonet against snow-covered mountains. The 171st has Northern Lights above the mountains and the 172nd has the Plough or Big Dipper.

173rd Airborne had a winged bayonet with a black Airborne tab above it. During the Vietnam War this patch appeared in modified forms reflecting both unit pride and anti-authoritarian attitudes. One version with inter-locked black and white fists bore the slogan 'Two Shades of Soul Togetherness', with 'The Herd' in place of the Airborne tab, while another retained 'The Herd' and re-placed the winged bayonet with a winged opium pipe.

A bayonet against the silhouette of a grenade and a bayonet on a white bar were adopted by the 191st Inf. Bde. in October 1963 and 193rd Inf. Bde. in August 1963 respectively.

The 196th Inf. Bde. has the double-headed slow fuse for a matchlock musket. The insignia was adopted in October 1965.

The 197th Inf. Bde. has a red cartridge against a blue and white background.

Among the heraldic motifs of the Artillery are the 30th Bde. raised on the Ryukyus Islands which has an oriental image of three arrows symbolizing three tens, within a circle. The 38th Artillery has a mailed fist on a red and yellow field, which symbolizes the divided Korean peninsula.

The 15th and 221st Military Police Bdes. both have Griffon's heads, similar in appearance to that of the 209th Field Artillery Bde.

A cross appears in the design of the 8th, 175th, 213th and 807th Medical Bde. patches. The 15th has an inverted sword with a swathing of bandages.

■ US ARMORED DIVISIONS ■

Currently there are five Armored Divisions in the US Army — the 1st, 2nd and 3rd are Active Army units while the 49th and 50th are divisions of the Army National Guard. All Armored Divisions have the triangular patch which was adopted by the Armored Corps in World War I. It is split into red, yellow and blue — the colors of the

1st Cavalry Division

1st Cavalry (non-standard woven patch produced to
commemorate the 1st Cav's airmobile role in Vietnam)

2nd Cavalry Division

75th Inf Brigade (subdued)

173rd Inf Brigade (without Airborne tab)

75th Field Artillery Brigade (subdued)

199th Inf Brigade

15th M.P. Brigade

cavalry, infantry and artillery — component parts of all armored formations.

The lightning bolt, tank tracks and cannon on round cavalry yellow patches were the insignia of the 1st Cavalry Regt. (Mech.), 7th Cav. Regt. (Mech.) and 13th Cav. Regt. (Mech.). Other units within the 7th Mechanized Cavalry Brigade, formed in 1937, had their arm colors as backing to the patch — so mechanized artillery and ordnance had red, and the medical troop, purple.

When the Armored Force was formed on July 10, 1940 its insignia, which was authorized on May 7, 1941, combined the triangular patch of the Armored Corps with that of the 7th Mechanized Cavalry Brigade in the center. Roman numerals were to have been positioned at the apex of each patch to distinguish each Corps. These were short-lived, with I Corps being disbanded after the landings in Sicily in 1943 and II, III, and IV Corps becoming the 18th, 19th and 20th Army Corps respectively. There were no V to XVIII Corps, though patches were made.

In World War II, Armored Division patches were made numbering from 1 to 22, though 17, 18, 19 and 21 did not exist. The National Guard Armored Divisions adopted numbers 27, 30, 40, 48, 49 and 50.

An M1 Abrams tank deployed on Reforger 82 in West Germany. The US Cavalry traded in their horses for tanks before World War II and the Abrams is the most modern MBT to enter service with Cavalry and Armored units.

The 1st Armd. Div. (Old Ironsides) fought in Europe in World War II and is an Active Army division with its HQ at Ansbach, West Germany, though the bulk of the division is at Fort Hood, in the US. Its equipment was used to reform the 1st Cavalry Div. in 1970-71 following the withdrawal of 1st Cav. from Vietnam. The 1st Armd. Div. in turn took on the equipment of the disbanded 4th.

The 2nd Armd. Div. (Hell on Wheels) fought in Europe in World War II and is an Active Army division based at Fort Hood, Texas after its return from Europe in 1946. It is the only armored division in the US Army to remain in continuous service since its activation. Under the command of General George S. Patton it earned its nickname 'Hell on Wheels'. It fought in the Battle of the Bulge after a 75-mile drive in ice and snow. As part of III Corps is returns to Europe on Reforger Exercises and was the first division to receive the M1 tank and Bradley fighting vehicle.

The 3rd Armd. Div. (Spearhead) fought in Europe. It is an active army unit which has been stationed in Frankfurt,

US Marines during peace-keeping operations in Lebanon wear a Stars and Stripes patch on their BDUs. The wearing of the national flag dates back to World War II, as the most obvious method of distinguishing US from other Allied forces.

West Germany since the 1950s.

The 49th Armd. Div. (Lone Star) has been called 'the largest division in NATO'. It is part of the Army National Guard based at Austin, Texas and was Federalized during the 1961 Berlin crisis. It has a star between the words 'Lone' and 'Star' on the title on its patch.

The 50th Armd. Div. (Jersey Blues) is part of the Army National Guard based at Somerset, New Jersey. Its divisional name is not displayed at the base of the patch as with the other armored divisions.

A prototype armored division is currently being planned for the US Army and it will be interesting to see which of the armored or cavalry divisions are reactivated for this role.

All the armored divisions fought in Europe in World War II. Their titles, which were largely embroidered with black letters on cavalry yellow, also appeared with yellow on khaki and blue with yellow letters. The titles reflect the violence and drive of armored warfare; 1st — Old Ironside, 2nd — Hell on Wheels, 3rd — Spearhead, 4th — Break-through, 5th — Victory, 6th — Super Sixth, 7th — Lucky 7th. The 8th was known as Iron Duce, Iron Snake and also Thundering Herd. The 9th changed from Phantom to Remagen after its successful *coup de main* at Remagen bridge on the Rhine in 1945. The 10th was known as Tiger, the 11th as Thunderbolt, the 12th as Hellcat, and also Speed is the Password, though whether this latter title appeared on a patch must beg the question of how it could be fitted in. The 13th was called Blackcat; the 14th, Liberator; the 27th, Empire and the 30th Dixie and Volunteers — the latter title is flanked by a miniature of the Roman XXX of the 30th Infantry Division. The 40th had the title Grizzly; the 48th, Hurricane; the 49th, Lone Star and the 50th, Jersey Blues.

The tricolored triangular armored patch also serves as the basis for armored personnel in GHQ, 3rd Armored Division Reconnaissance, with the letters RCN, Demonstration Regiment — DR, 7th Army Tank Training Center — TTC, 17th Armored Group — 17GP, 510th Armored Reconnaissance Battalion — 510 RECON, 7th Cavalry Regiment — 7 CAV. The most fascinating is the patch worn by a special armored unit which was in training for the invasion of Japan — it was an unnumbered armor patch with an Airborne tab above it.

ABOVE The 2nd Armd. Div. — Hell on Wheels — on
Exercise Certain Strike, part of Reforger 87. A Spec 4 in
the turret of his M1 Abrams main battle tank.

TOP Dressed in camouflaged BDUs (battle dress utilities),
a US Army officer talks to a Dutch officer. The subdued US
Army Vietnam patch can be seen on his right shoulder
indicating service in Vietnam.

CHAPTER FOUR

OPERATIONAL THEATERS, COMMANDS, SUPPORT SERVICES AND TRAINING SCHOOLS

US Army medics work on a casualty on Utah Beach on June 6, 1944. They have the universally recognised Red Cross insignia, though the divisional patch on the casualty (who is also a medic) has been removed by the censor.

■ THEATERS, COMMANDS ■ AND SUPPORT SERVICES

During World War II a range of patches was produced for the different war theaters, commands and training establishments. Often, these were as symbolic as many of the heraldic devices on divisional patches.

The Army Ground Forces included representations of the Armored Corps patch for the Armored Center, a glider and parachute for the Airborne Command, and the British Combined Operations motif of Eagle, Anchor and Tommy Gun for Amphibious Forces. The British design was in red on a black background.

US Army Amphibious Units adopted the patch in yellow on blue, while Combined Operations retained the original design. A ship's wheel on a red shield was used for Ports of Embarkation. The Engineer Amphibious Command had a small seahorse within an oval patch, while Bomb Disposal had a aircraft bomb shape similar to the British patch. Tank destroyer units had a snarling black panther flanked by tracks. Without the tracks and slightly modified, the motif was to reappear as the patch of the Vietnamese Rangers (Biet Dong Ouan) in the 1960s and 70s.

The Frontier Defense Sectors were manned by the coastal artillery and had a series of patches in red and yellow on a khaki background. These included the 1st Coastal Artillery (New England), 2nd (New York — Philadelphia), 3rd (Chesapeake Bay), 4th (Southern Coastal) and 9th (Pacific Coastal). Hawaii, which after Pearl Harbor was more threatened than the mainland US seaboard, had two patches for Coastal Defense and the Coastal Artillery Brigade. Anti-aircraft Defense had patches using the same colors but with arrows in place of the shell motif. The Anti-Aircraft Command had the letters 'AA' in red on white within a blue bordered circle. There were AA Artillery Commands for the Central, Southern and Eastern United States.

The Army Ground Forces had a simple circular patch in red, white and blue and yellow, red and blue for the Replacement and School Command. The Army Service Forces (ASF) had a blue star within a white octofoil patch with a red border. The ASF provided service and support for the army both in the United States and later overseas.

The World War II patch of US Armed Forces Pacific Ocean Area theater depicted the twelve stars of the Southern Cross constellation. The Southern Cross on its own was adopted by US Army Forces in the South Atlantic — however this patch also included the silhouette of Ascension Island rising from a green ocean.

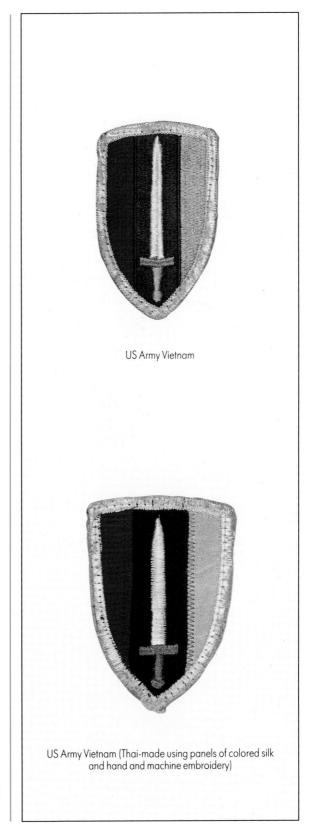

US Army Vietnam

US Army Vietnam (Thai-made using panels of colored silk and hand and machine embroidery)

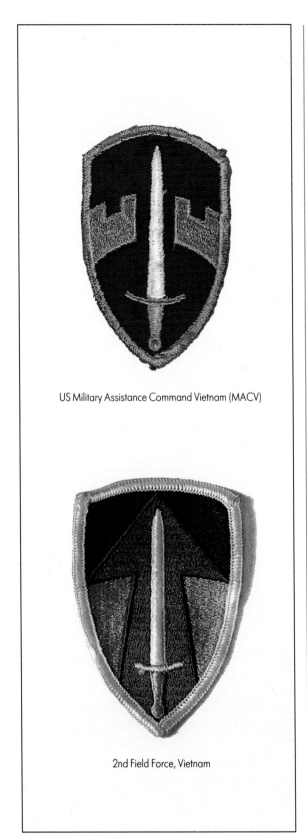

US Military Assistance Command Vietnam (MACV)

2nd Field Force, Vietnam

The ETO — European Theater of Operations — had two patches. Both featured an arrow bursting through chains symbolizing Nazi occupation. The Advanced Base patch had within it a miniature of the Army Service Forces patch.

A Moorish dome enclosing a star was adopted for North Africa. Perhaps the most widely known theater patch is the CBI — China-Burma-India — shield with its Nationalist Chinese sun and US star. It is a patch often associated with leather flight jackets of the US Flying Tigers pilots who operated in support of the Nationalist Chinese forces. The 5307th Composite Unit, widely known as Merrill's Marauders which operated in Burma with British and Chinese, forces also used the Sun and Star design. There were a number of patches which also included a red lightning bolt on a shield quartered in blue and black. The CBI patch was to survive after the War as the MAAG Formosa patch, with the letters MAAG in place of the US star. Men working on the Ledo or Burma road had a patch depicting the road winding through mountains towards a Chinese sun, above on a red bar were three stars. US forces in the Middle East had a star on a red field above two wavy blue lines.

The Supreme Headquarters Allied Expeditionary Forces, worn in North West Europe by personnel on General Eisenhower's staff, showed a flaming sword penetrating the darkness of Occupied Europe with a rainbow band of color and a pale blue band. After the War the design was retained for the US Army Europe, but dark blue was substituted for black. With the tab 'Berlin' it was worn by the Berlin Brigade. The sword and rainbow appeared in the patch of the US Military Liaison Mission Potsdam, though with the addition of the Stars and Stripes.

Allied Forces HQ had the letters 'AF' on a blue circle, with a red border. The General HQ South West Pacific showed the letters 'GHQ' on a standard against a khaki field.

The US Mission to Moscow had a representation of the American eagle and shield with 'America' in cyrilic script above it.

Base and Defense commands were respectively located overseas and in the US. Base commands were to protect the United States in war, though the London Base Command, which featured Big Ben and the letters 'LBC', was principally involved in work on the Second Front.

The Iceland Base Command showed an iceberg with the tip showing red above the sea; the Greenland Command, sea and ice in blue and white lines. The Caribbean Defense Command showing a galleon in full sail lives on as the 33rd Infantry Combat team patch with the tab 33rd Infantry. The same patch with the tab 'Jungle Ex-

Military Advisory Assistance Group — Laos (also produced in black)

US Army Special Forces

Special Forces (subdued)

Airborne, Recondo and Special Forces tabs in full color and subdued.

MACV (subdued)

China, Burma, India Theater (modern copy).

US TASCOM Europe

Ledo Road (WWII)

US Army Europe

Military District of Washington (WWII)

A 155mm self-propelled gun is used against a German bunker on the Siegfried line in November 1944. The impact of the big shells with super quick fuzes was devastating when they hit the bunkers.

pert' is awarded to men who have completed the course run by the Jungle Warfare Training Center at Fort Sherman, Panama Canal Zone, which was set up in the 1950s. With the colors reversed as a blue ship on a white patch the same design was adopted by the School of the Americas — the US sponsored civil and military training establishment for officers from Central and South America.

The Military District of Washington patch is oval with the Washington Memorial and a red sword. It was part of the Army Service Forces.

Men attending the Officers Candidates School had a simple patch with the letters 'S' and 'C' interlocked and enclosed by an 'O'. The Army Specialized Training Program and Reserve trained young men in colleges and schools. The Reserve Officers Training Corps, ROTC, had three patches. The first design was a shield, changed in the 1950s to a red, white and blue patch with the torch of knowledge. The current design has a sword against a representation of classical columns. Since the war ROTCs have developed a range of individual college patches.

In World War II there were individual commands which included the US Army in Alaska, where troops wore patches with polar bears and seals. The rather attractive cartoon seal on the Alaskan Defense Command, with the Aurora Borealis, was changed to a more aggressive snarling polar bear when the Command was transformed into a Department.

The Antilles Department had a turret from a Spanish fort in red and yellow, the colors of the Spanish flag. The Panama Department had the portcullis of the Panama Hellgate and a shield device suggesting the isthmus that joins North and South America. The Philippine Department had an armed sealion, and Hawaii an 'H' configured like an Oriental *mon*.

After World War II, occupation produced its own patches. The Berlin District had the Brandenburg Gate on an orange shield. Troops in Trieste, the disputed port on the Italian/Yugoslav border, had a modified version of the 88th Division patch with the town crest in the center and a tab reading 'Trust' above it. US troops in Austria had the Tactical Command patch and the US Forces

Brass on parade — their patches are either European
(Advanced Base) or S.H.A.E.F. The officers in the front
row have several medals and overseas service stripes
and even the wound stripes from World War I on their cuffs.

Austria, which used the Austrian colors of red and white
with a sword and a branch of laurel. There were two
versions, one with the words 'Austria' and 'US' on a
square patch, the other without letters on a classic shield
shape. One of the more intriguing patches is the US
Allied Control Command Hungary — this was a shield
with the words 'America US ACC Magyarorszag'.

The US TASCOM Europe, which was set up in France
on April 25, 1953, features a French fleur-de-lis and an
arrow representing the flow of supplies. On August 6,
1964 it was renamed US Army Communications Zone,
Europe and on September 26, 1969 it became US Theater
Army Support Command, Europe.

The war crimes trials in Japan and Nuremberg, Germany
produced their own patches. Both featured the scales of
justice, though the Japanese trials had in addition a
lightning bolt crossed with an oriental sword.

US Forces in the Far East had a circular patch showing
a snow-capped Mt Fuji, topped off with a black tab
'29th RCT Raiders' when the patch was later used by the

29th Regimental Combat Team. The Ryukus Command
based in Okinawa had a yellow Torii gate on a black
patch. The Japan Logistics Command had the letters 'JLC'
in a mock Oriental script, while the West Pacific Far East
Command adopted the wartime Army Service Forces
patch with a lightning bolt and five smaller stars like the
Southern Cross. Guam base had two patches, the first
had the word 'Guam' on a patch showing a palm tree
and a sailing boat. When the Mariannas, Bonin, Guam
Command was formed the patch was changed to a
single palm tree — perhaps the old patch was a little too
like an image from a holiday brochure.

The growth of US involvement in South East Asia after
World War II produced patches for the Military Assistance
Advisory Group, MAAG. It was a blue patch with twelve
white stars and resembled the 508th Airborne Infantry
Regiment patch, except that the 508th was based on the
82nd Airborne patch with a red square and an Airborne
tab. There were MAAGs in Laos, Formosa, Thailand and
Vietnam. In Vietnam the increase in US involvement in
the 1960s and the creation of the Military Assistance
Command, Vietnam, MACV, produced a patch showing
a white sword on a red shield breaking through an arched
'embattled fess' — a heraldic fortified wall. MACV pro-

Pacific Ocean Area (WWII)

European (Advanced Base) (WWII)

Aleutian Islands Command

North Africa (WWII)

US Army Forces Western Pacific

Berlin District

Alaska Support Command

Army Amphibian Units (WWII)

Airborne Command

1st Allied Airborne Army

1st Special Service Force

Army Ground Forces

A Lieutenant of Engineers (the castle insignia is on his coat) with the shoulder patch of the Army Service Forces on his jacket admires a Renoir in the Louvre.

Army Service Forces

Replacement and School Command

Anti-aircraft Command

duced a *Staff Memorandum 670-1* which read: 'Yellow and red are the Republic of Vietnam colors. The red ground alludes to the infiltration and oppression from beyond the embattled wall (i.e. The Great Wall of China). The opening in the wall through which this infiltration and oppression flow is blocked by the sword representing US military aid and support. The wall is arched and the sword pointed upward in reference to the offensive action pushing the aggressor back.'

The US Army Vietnam adopted a shield divided vertically into yellow, blue and red with a sword in the central blue section. Yellow and red were the colors of the Republic of Vietnam, though some observers talked about the yellow and red 'hordes' of North Vietnam and China. The 1st and 2nd Field Force in Vietnam had variants of the US Army Vietnam patch. The three colors were common to both as was the vertical sword, though 1st Field Force had a battle-axe-shaped patch and the 2nd incorporated a blue arrow thrusting into a red field.

Officers and men of the 82nd Airborne arrive in Paris for
R and R in World War II. The man second from the left has
paratrooper's wings on his tunic. The men have the patch
of glider-borne paratroops on their forage caps. Their
high Corcoran boots further identify them as paratroops.

Vietnam saw the growth of informal patches for divisional sniper and reconnaissance teams and even commemorative patches, like the one produced for men who
participated in the Son Tay raid on November 21, 1970.
The Special Forces, with their distinctive green beret and
its colored cloth badge backings and 'Saigon Electrical
Works' patch of a sword with three lightning bolts,
achieved a considerable military cachet and sense of
mystique in the South-East Asian theater.

With patches came a variety of shoulder tabs in colors
which imitated the prized Ranger tab. Some said simply
'Sniper', 'Commando', 'Scout Dog', 'Scout', 'Tracker' or
'Combat Artists', though others boasted 'Sons of
Bitche', 'Sheep', 'Clowns' or, rather chillingly, 'Funeral

Squad'. Kit Carson Scouts, Vietcong or North Vietnamese
who had surrendered to the US Army and opted to join
them as scouts, had their own patch.

Helicopter airmobility in Vietnam produced variants on
some older cavalry patches as 1st Cavalry became 'Airmobile'. The patches, as with other 'informal' insignia,
were usually worn on the left pocket. There are over 200
recorded specialist or 'elite' patches and insignia gener-
ated by the Vietnam War and they have been the subject
of books in their own right.

■ SCHOOLS, TRAINING ■ CENTERS AND TRAINING COURSES

The Military Academy at West Point is probably the most
widely known training establishment in the US Army. Its

Army Materiel Command

1st Logistical Command

Army Reserve Officers Training Corps

Combat Developments Command

Engineer Center and School

Corps of Engineers

Infantry School

Jungle School (cadre) (subdued)

O.C.S. (Female)

Aviation School

Signal Corps Center and School

Caribbean Defence Command

An officer and a gentleman — Officer-Cadet Hunn and his partner at the Class of 1970 'Ring Hop' at the West Point Military Academy. The giant ring represents the Academy Graduation ring favored by officers in the US Army — as such it is an informal item of insignia.

patch features a classical Greek helmet on a gray and black shield. Two versions exist: the cadre patch has an oblique black bar, while the US Military Academy has the shield divided into quarters.

A man's cotton shirt, sateen OG 107 with a DSA number indicating a manufacture date in 1967 in the author's collection has an interesting combination of patches. The owner, Lt Moran, an infantry officer in the 199th Inf. Brigade (Light), served operationally in Vietnam where the Brigade was deployed between 1966 and 1970. He won the Combat Infantry Badge. Most intriguingly he then went to serve on the cadre of the US Military Academy — presumably as an experienced young infantry officer on the administrative staff. The shirt is also unusual in having a subdued inked name tag, subdued embroidered rank and CIB, but an earlier black and gold US Army tab and full color patches.

Before any training can be undertaken by a soldier he has to be recruited or drafted into the army. The US Army Recruiting Service initially had a shield-shaped patch which was later changed to a square and then to

Civil Affairs School (subdued)

Field Artillery School

Recruiting Command

A different sort of insignia — OPFOR, the pseudo-soviet forces who are the enemy at the National Training Center, Fort Irwin, California. They have characteristic black berets and insignia like that of the Soviet Army — the vehicle is a modified Sheridan light tank.

A photographer of the US Army Combat Pictorial Division with the Strategic Communications Command patch adjusts his equipment during an exercise in 1988. As a lower priority unit he has not yet reached the Kevlar 'Fritz' helmet and so still wears the GI 'pot'.

an oval design. The square and oval patches show the Liberty Bell surrounded by the 13 stars of the first States of the Union.

Staff and students at training establishments in the United States, Europe and Asia had patches which indicated that they were either graduates or part of the training team. Patches or tabs fostered a mystique and a competitive edge. The Infantry School has a bayonet on an infantry blue background with the motto 'Follow Me'.

The US Intelligence Command has the Sphinx on a pale blue background, while the Intelligence Agency has a rose in blue and gray. The rose is also used by the British Army Intelligence Corps. The US Army Engineer Technical Intelligence Team has the castle of the Corps of Engineers. The Field Artillery School has a vertical view of a cannon on a red shield. The Artillery and Missile School

has the black outline of a missile superimposed on the shield. The Army War College has the torch of knowledge on a black shield with three stars; the Command and General Staff School, Fort Leavenworth, has three oil lamps with an inverted 'V'.

The patch which attracted most sarcastic comment was the Special Warfare School insignia, which was likened to a cooking pot. It is a shield with a three-flamed lamp backed by the crossed arrows of the Special Forces.

The Fixed Wing Aviation and Helicopter Schools have, respectively, a blue shield with a red observation aircraft, and a red shield with a black Sikorsky helicopter. The Aviation School has a winged torch, similar in design to the 173rd Airborne and 1st Aviation Brigade.

The Judge Advocate General School has a sword and quill pen with the torch and laurel wreath. The Civil

Tank Destroyer Forces

Special Warfare School

107th Transportation Brigade

107th A.C.R

67th Inf Brigade

197th Inf Brigade

Affairs School patch features a sword and scroll.

The 'Enemy' force for soldiers in training centers in the 1950s in the United States was originally composed of men in the 'Aggressor Force'. They had a patch showing a green triangle inside a circle. Following Vietnam, there was a serious re-evaluation of training and Opposing Forces, or OPFOR, were established at the National Training Center, Fort Irwin. OPFOR wear a version of Soviet uniforms and use real Eastern Bloc or modified US vehicles. They have a patch showing a black star on a green circle. Staff at the National Training Center have a patch which has the red, yellow and blue of artillery, cavalry and infantry.

A diamond in Army or Corps colors, with the torch of knowledge and Corps insignia or a version of it, has been adopted by ten US Army Centers and Schools. They are: Missile & Munitions, Military Intelligence, Military Police, Ordnance, Chemical Corps, Transportation, Medical, Quartermaster, Signal Corps and Engineer.

Specialized units and training courses run at divisional level often feature a variation of the divisional patch. However, the 2nd Infantry Division Rangers School features a map of Korea with the North in red and South in white. A Spec 4s OD shirt in the author's collection has the shirt pocket patch with the 2nd Division Indian head on the left sleeve. The Ranger Patch features an Indian head on an arrow pointing northward with the motto 'Imjin Scouts'. The 5th Division Recondo School has a black Roman 'V' with the motto 'Recondo'.

2nd Infantry come ashore in Korea in 1963. The Indian Head Division has been resident in Korea since the end of the Korean War.

Selection of subdued tabs. The USATC is the US Army Training Center, while the River Patrol Boat operated in Vietnam.

7th Transport Brigade

The cadre patch for the US Military Academy West Point on the right sleeve of Lt Moran's shirt.

CHAPTER FIVE

THE UNITED STATES ARMY AIR FORCE

A USAAF B-17 bomber with nose art of the Commander
in Chief of the Allied Forces—Ike.

A Staff Sergeant of the US Army Air Force 9th Air Force turns on the charm with the mother of his Parisian date in 1944.

Prior to 1947, when the USAF was established as a separate force, it was, as the United States Army Air Force, part of the US Army. It had begun life in 1907 as three men in the Army Signal Corps. In 1926 it was designated the Air Corps, having earned its wings in World War I. In World War II the Corps was reorganized in June 1941 and was designated the Army Air Force. The 1st, 2nd, 3rd and 4th Air Forces were Continental Air Forces which were tasked with the defense of the United States. The Combat Air Forces were activated in strategic areas of operation and their unit patches were to become the outward signs of the USAAF's overseas power projection.

The old USAAF patch was an oriental-style design which also resembled a turning propellor blade. The 'new' patch used the pre-War USAAF white star with a circular center which was painted on USAAF aircraft. The patch had a blue background with yellow wings. Most of the USAAF patches were circular on a blue background; exceptions were the 2nd Air Force (square), the 6th (six sided), the 11th (shield), the 12th (inverted triangle), the

US Strategic Air Force and the Desert Air Force (shields).

The 1st Air Force had the figure '1' above the patch, the 2nd an eagle with a star, the 3rd a figure '3', the 4th a winged star and four radiating gold bars. The 5th had five stars, with the figure '5' and the star as a meteor. It was originally the Philippine Department Air Force and was activated in May 1941. It was redesignated the 5th Air Force in 1942 and supported landings on Guadalcanal and Admiralty Islands and saw air action in New Guinea.

The 6th, which had a winged star with the silhouette of a galleon above it, was the Panama Canal Air Force. It was responsible for defense of the strategically-important Canal Zone and for anti-submarine operations in the Gulf of Mexico. The galleon motif has remained in use in the US Army.

The 7th had a star pierced by a figure '7'. It originated as the Hawaiian Air Force and was redesignated the 7th

1st Air Force

3rd Air Force

in February 1942. It covered the Hawaiian Islands and became the principal striking force in the Central Pacific.

The 8th, 'The Mighty 8th', was the striking force against Germany and Occupied Europe and was based in the United Kingdom. Its B-17 bombers and Mustang fighters made deep penetration raids into Germany. It had a winged '8' which enclosed the USAAF star.

The 9th had the figure '9' in red on a gold circle with white wings topped by the USAAF star. The 9th was activated in April 1942 and served in the Middle East. After the North African campaign it was transferred to the United Kingdom to support operations in Europe. The 9th became one of the largest Tactical Air Forces in the world.

The 10th had the figure '10' with gold wings topped by the USAAF star. The 10th was activated in 1942 and operated against Japanese supply lines in Burma and in the defense of China and India.

The 11th Air Force had the figure '11' with a USAAF star with a single wing. The 11th, which had been the Alaskan Air Force, was redesignated in February 1942. It saw action in the North Pacific at Dutch Harbor, the Aleutian Islands and in long-range bombing missions against the Kurile Islands.

The 12th had the figure '12' within a winged star. It was activated in August 1942 and operated as a Tactical Air Force in support of ground troops in North Africa and the invasion of Europe.

The 13th had a winged star with '13' above. Activated in January 1943 it provided air defense of supply routes in the South Pacific and tactical air support of land and sea operations in the Solomon Islands.

The 14th was known as the China Air Task Force and, before that, The Flying Tigers. They sported a winged tiger with the USAAF star. The 14th was activated in July 1942 under command of the 10th and then became an Air Force in its own right in March 1943. It was tasked with the defense of China and with attacks on Japanese lines of communication in Burma.

The 15th had a patch similar to the 13th, but had the figure '15' in yellow thread. It was activated in November 1943 as a strategic Air Force in the Mediterranean Allied Air Force. It was involved in long-range bombing operations against Germany.

RIGHT Following the airborne assault in the Rhine crossings, a US paratrooper with the bayonet fixed on his Garand moves towards a billowing cargo parachute.

5th Air Force

7th Air Force

9th Air Force

13th Air Force

Airborne Troop Carrier

11th Air Force

The 20th had a globe motif over the winged star and figure '20'. It was activated in 1944 for very long-range strategic bombing operations in the Far East against Japan. There were also tactical or strategic Air Forces within Area of Operation Air Forces. They were joint commands by the USAAF or British RAF.

The Desert Air Force had a winged 8th Army shield with a bar bearing an RAF roundel and USAAF star. The 9th and 12th Air Forces operated in conjunction with the RAF in North Africa.

The Mediterranean Allied Air Force grew out of the Desert Air Force and the 12th Air Force and was tasked with supporting the invasion of Sicily. The patch was an unusual shape, being four-sided, with white wings above the letters MAAF on wavy pale blue lines.

The US Strategic Air Force Europe was activated in January 1944, combining the 8th and 15th Air Forces into a powerful force in the long-range war against Germany. It had a shield-shaped patch with a winged star and the letters 'USSTAF'.

The Air Training Command grew out of the amalgamation of the Technical Training Command and the Flying Training Command in July 1943. The patch consisted of a winged white star pierced by the torch of knowledge. The Air Transport Command, activated in April 1941 as the Ferry Command, was redesignated in 1942 and had two sections, Ferrying and Air Transport. The patch showed a half globe, but did not have the USAAF star. A separate gold-colored patch was produced for Air Transport Command Ground Personnel.

Troop Carrier Command had a huge eagle carrying an armed man. Its role was to train troop carrier and glider crews, and the evacuation of the wounded.

The Airborne Troop Carrier had a shield incorporating the Airborne tab as well as the words 'Troop Carrier' and a USAAF star suspended on a parachute with wings. It transported airborne forces and stores in combat.

Perhaps one of the most fascinating patches was that for The Manhattan Project, the secret project to build the atomic bomb which was under the command of USAAF General Groves. It shows a gold atom being split by a white bolt coming from another which bears the USAAF star.

Specialists had blue inverted triangle patches which showed a camera (Air Force Photography Specialist), a wind vane (AF Weather Specialist), a gear wheel (AF Engineering Specialist), a radio mast (AF Communications Specialist) and a bomb (AF Armature Specialist).

US Army Air Force

USAAF 8th Air Force

SECTION TWO

MEDALS AND DECORATIONS

CHAPTER SIX

FOR VALOR

It is, perhaps, not surprising, that the first award of honor for the common soldier, rather than for high-ranking military elites, was given in the United States, where the idea of equality of all men was a guiding principle. The Continental Congress had passed resolutions awarding medals to officers of the Army and Navy for victories during the War of Independence. These were large table-top medals not intended for wear. The first such medal was authorized on March 25, 1776 and presented to General George Washington for forcing the enemy evacuation of Boston on March 17, 1776. Five further medals were awarded in subsequent years.

The next three medals awarded were unique, for they were presented to enlisted men rather than officers, and also they were created by Congress with the specific understanding that they were to be worn as decorations by the recipients.

These were the so-called "Andre" medals, given to the three American militiamen, John Paulding, Isaac Van Wart and David Williams who captured the British intelligence agent Major Andre carrying dispatches from General Benedict Arnold involving his plot to betray the American cause.

The three New York Militiamen were each presented with a brace of pistols with silver mounts by General Washington. He also presented the medals to them and read the resolution of Congress thanking them for their high sense of virtuous and patriotic conduct, and ordering them to receive 200 dollars annually during their life. The medals were made by a silversmith in New York and two of them are now in the possession of the New York Historical Society. This was the first award of a military medal to an enlisted man or common soldier.

Two years later, on August 7, 1782, Washington created the Badge of Military Merit. In his Order of the Day establishing the Badge of Military Merit, Washington issued the following directive:

AZTEC CLUB OF 1847

The General . . . directs that whenever any singular meritorious action is performed, the author of it shall be permitted to wear on his facing, over the left breast, the figure of a heart of purple cloth, or silk, edged with narrow lace or binding . . .

Unfortunately, this award, the first of its kind in military history, was allowed to fall into disuse at the close of the War. Although it may have been awarded on other occasions, there have been only three known recipients:

BADGE OF MILITARY MERIT

ANDRE MEDAL,
(Obverse)

MEXICAN WAR VETERANS BADGE

Sergeant Elijah Churchill, 2nd Regiment Light Dragoons, awarded the badge for raids on Fort St. George, Long Island; Sergeant William Brown, 5th Connecticut Regiment, for heroic actions at Yorktown on October 14, 1781; and Sergeant Daniel Bissell, 2nd Connecticut Regiment, for continued intelligence and information behind the British lines in Staten Island, New York City and Long Island during 1782.

Except for these awards, no recognition was given to the hundreds of brave men in the Revolution, in the War of 1812, in the Mexican War, and the early wars with the Indians in the West. They were the unsung heroes.

On May 13 1783 at the close of hostilities in the War of the Revolution for American Independence in the cantonments of the Continental Army on the Hudson, American and French officers came together to hold the first meeting of the newly created historic and patriotic Order of the Cincinnati founded in remembrance of their allied service during the conflict.

Membership in this Society was open to all officers of the Continental Army who served honorably during the war. A distinctive badge of membership was designed and made available to the members on May 5, 1784.

■ THE FIRST ■ CAMPAIGN MEDALS

The idea of the Order led to the creation of others, some of them fraternal and others formed by veterans of wars and campaigns, such as the Military Society of the War of 1812 and the Aztec Club of 1847.

The Mexican War, 1846–1848, saw the founding of the Aztec Club (actually inaugurated in the captured capital of Mexico City on Octobr 13, 1847), open to officers of the military who fought in the War. Also created during this period was a new type of veterans group called the Mexican War Veterans Association, which was open to both officers and enlisted veterans of the war. Both groups issued a member's badge.

Different states also issued medals to state residents who served during this War. Medals to the Palmetto Regiment of South Carolina, the New York State Volunteers and Scott's Legion of Philadelphia were added to the growing list of badges and medals being worn by Americans to indicate military service.

Another award created during this period was the

**A DIPLOMA OF THE SOCIETY
OF
CINCINNATI, 1785**

Certificate of Merit, established by Congress on March 3, 1847, in an act to establish a system of awards and offer brevet, honory rank without pay, commissions as Second Lieutenants to non-commissioned officers who distinguish themselves as recommended by their regimental commanders. The act also provided that when any private soldier should similarly distinguish himself, the President might grant him a certificate of merit entitling him to two dollars per month additional pay.

The original certificates issued for the Mexican War were large documents, engraved on parchment and signed by the President and Secretary of War. A total of 545 men received Certificates of Merit for conspicuous service during the Mexican War. In 1854, noncommissioned officers were made eligible for this award. A total of 1,206 soldiers received the Certificate of Merit during the seventy-one years of its existence.

■ THE CIVIL WAR ■

With the outbreak of the Civil War on April 12, 1861 a series of new medals and awards came into existence, including medals issued by several states to the men who volunteered for war service after President Lincoln's call for troops. These men were called "the First Defenders"

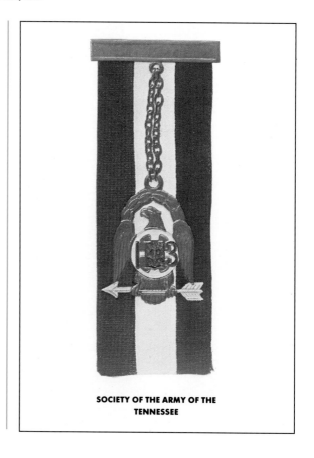

**SOCIETY OF THE ARMY OF THE
TENNESSEE**

FOR VALOR ■

SOUTHERN CROSS OF HONOR
This highly honored badge was awarded by the
Daughters of the Confederacy and is quite rare.
The bar at the top of the badge has the name of
the recipient engraved upon it.

**MILITARY SOCIETY OF THE ARMY OF THE POTOMAC
BADGE**
This badge was worn by members of the society
that was created after the Civil War, 1861–65. It
was composed of officers who served in this unit
during any of its campaigns during the war.

or the "Minutemen of 1861" and the medals were so inscribed. These medals were issued by Connecticut, Massachusetts, New Jersey and Pennsylvania. In addition, the states of New Jersey, New York, Maryland, Ohio and West Virginia and the City of Brooklyn, New York issued medals for service during the Civil War.

A number of decorations were created within the Army during the War. Because of the small number presented, these medals are quite rare, and they are all unofficial. These include the Kearny Medal created on November 29, 1862 and the Second style Kearny Cross created on March 13, 1863, awarded by the Third Division, Army of the Potomac.

Veterans of the Army of the Confederate States also had some unofficial decorations, including the Davis Guard Medal for the battle of Sabine Pass, Texas on September 8, 1863. Two of the most famous medals of the Confederate States were struck and issued years after the War ended. These were The Southern Cross of Honor created by the Daughters of the Confederacy and awarded to Confederate Veterans in 1898, and the New Market Cross of Honor created in 1904 by the Alumni Association of the Virginia Military Institute to honor the VMI Cadets who fought at the battle of New Market, Virginia on May 15, 1864.

Following the earlier custom of creating societies to perpetuate the memories of service, the veterans of both sides created a number of Military Societies after the War. Some of these were: The Army of the Cumberland; Army of Georgia; Army of the James; Army of the Potomac; Army of the Tennessee; Army of West Virginia; Army of North Virginia and the Army and Navy of the Gulf.

The largest of these groups, The Grand Army of the Republic (GAR), was open to anyone who saw Federal service during the War, and over the years created hundreds of different badges. The GAR was to become very involved with the Medal of Honor in the years to come: in fact, most recommendations for the medal for service during the Civil War took place during the many State and National Conventions of this group. On the other side was the Confederate Veterans Association.

85

**THE SOCIETY OF THE ARMY OF
THE JAMES**

**THE SOCIETY OF THE ARMY OF
WEST VIRGINIA**

**THE SOCIETY OF THE ARMY OF
THE CUMBERLAND**

MASSACHUSETTS MINUTE MAN OF 1861 MEDAL

CONNECTICUT FIRST DEFENDERS MEDAL,
April 15, 1861

CHAPTER SEVEN

THE BEGINNING OF
THE PYRAMID OF HONOR

Senator James Grimes of Iowa, who was Chairman of the Senate Naval Committee, took an interest in awards, and introduced a bill in Congress to promote the efficiency of the Navy.

On December 21, 1861 President Abraham Lincoln signed this bill, Public Resolution 82, into law. Section 7 of the Act provided that, "The Secretary of the Navy be, and is hereby, authorized to cause two hundred medals of honor to be prepared with suitable emblematic devices which shall be bestowed upon such petty officers, seamen, landsmen and marines as shall distinguish themselves by their gallantry in action and other seamanlike qualities during the present war . . ."

This bill was a landmark in the history of United States decorations and medals.

▓ THE FIRST MEDAL ▓
OF HONOR

The Navy Medal of Honor, which was (in the modern sense) the first federal decoration, was designed by Christian Schussel and sculptured by Anthony C. Paquet.

The design of the first medal is indictive of the fact that it was created for the Civil War only, with little thought that it would continue after the War. James Pollock, the director of the United States Mint where the medal was made, described in a letter dated May 9, 1862 to Secretary of the Navy, Gideon Welles, the scene on the obverse as one in which, "the foul spirit of secession and rebellion is represented in a crouching attitude holding in his hands, serpents, which with forked tongues are striking at a large figure representing the Union or Genius of our country, who holds in right hand a shield and in her left the fasces. Around these figures are thirty-four stars, indicating the number of states composing the Union."

This design is in the center of an inverted five-pointed star with laurel leaves and a trefoil at each point. At the

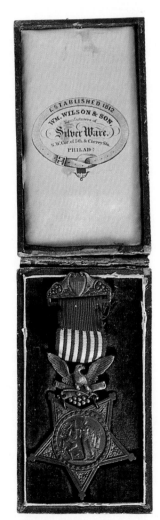

Army Medal of Honor, First design in original case. Name of the recipient was typed and glued to the back of the case, when the medal was issued.

top of the star is a hanger in the form of an anchor, entwined with a cable, indicating the naval service. On February 17, 1862, Senator Henry Wilson of Massachusetts introduced a Senate Resolution proposing a similar medal of honor for enlisted men of the Army. The Resolution was amended on March 3, 1863 to allow commissioned officers of the Army to receive the medal and to make gallantry in action the sole qualification for the Army Medal of Honor.

At the suggestion of Secretary of the Navy Welles, it was decided that the Army would use the same basic design for their medal that was used for the Navy Medal of Honor, with some slight modifications.

The pin clasp and suspension device were changed. The Army medal was suspended from the ribbon by a trophy composed of crossed cannons above eight stacked cannon balls and a sabre. At the top of the trophy is an eagle with extended wings with a loop in the rear, through which the ribbon passes. The top bar is composed of a shield between two cornucopia symbolizing America as the land of plenty.

Both the design of the Medal of Honor, and the laws which govern it have been changed many times over the years. These changes and, where possible, the reasons the design was altered, are listed below.

THE NAVY MEDAL OF HONOR
(1861–1913)

Authorized on December 12, 1861. The medal was awarded to petty officers, seamen, landsmen and marines for gallantry in action and other seamanlike qualities (such as the saving of lives). Officers were not eligible until March 3, 1915, but some awards were made retro-active to earlier campaigns.

This design was used from December 21, 1861 to August 11, 1913. The reverse of the medal is inscribed with the words, "Personal Valor" to be followed by the name of the recipient, his rank, ship, and the place and date of the deed for which the medal was awarded.

THE ARMY MEDAL OF HONOR
(1862–1896)

Authorized on July 12, 1862 it remained in use for thirty-four years, until 1896. It was presented to Army non-commissioned officers and privates for gallantry in action and other soldier-like qualities. Officers were made eligible for the award on March 3, 1863.

ARMY MEDAL OF HONOR
(SECOND DESIGN, 1896–1904)

Authorized on May 2, 1896, creating a new ribbon design for the Army Medal of Honor, which also authorized the Secretary of War to issue the new ribbon to those who held a Medal of Honor. There was no change in the design of the medal, but the medal suspension was attached to a neck cravat and was to be worn at the neck.

■ SAFEGUARDS OF ■ INTEGRITY

Many of the Civil War Veteran's organizations and other patriotic societies formed after the war issued members badges that looked like the Medal of Honor. The largest veterans group, The Grand Army of the Republic, the GAR, had a member's badge that was really a thinly disguised replica of the Medal of Honor, even to the ribbon design. It was hoped that the new ribbon design would deal with this problem.

In spite of the change in ribbon design, the Army Medal of Honor continued to be widely copied. It was decided by the Medal of Honor Legion, a group composed of holders of the medal, that a completely new design of the medal was necessary.

At the same time, actions were being taken to protect the medal and impose a time limit requirement for sub-mitting applications for the medal. Hundreds of medals had been awarded forty years after actions that took place during the Civil War.

This led to an Act of Congress approved on April 23, 1904, creating a time limit for recommendations and making it mandatory that all claims for the Medal should be accompanied by official documents describing the deed involved.

A new design was approved and the patent for the new Medal of Honor was then assigned to "W.H. Taft and his successor or successors as Secretary of War of the United States of America", thus halting uncontrolled imitations of the Medal of Honor.

ARMY MEDAL OF HONOR
(THIRD DESIGN, 1904–1944)

Authorized on April 23, 1904. The Army's highest award for gallantry in action, the Medal of Honor is awarded for extraordinary gallantry and intrepidity at the risk of their lives above and beyond the call of duty against an armed enemy of the United States. A ribbon of light blue moire

NAVY MEDAL OF HONOR
(1861–1913)

ARMY MEDAL OF HONOR,
(1862–1896)

ARMY MEDAL OF HONOR,
Second design (1896–1904)

NAVY MEDAL OF HONOR,
Third style (1917–1942)

NAVY MEDAL OF HONOR,
Second style (1913–1917)

ARMY MEDAL OF HONOR,
Third design (1904–1944)

with thirteen white stars was also approved with the new design.

When the new medals were produced, holders of the Old style Medal of Honor, could request the new Medal, and the new medal, engraved with the full details on the back would be issued to the recipient when he "traded in" or surrendered the old one.

On September 20, 1905, an Executive order of President Theodore Roosevelt, provided that the presentation of a Medal of Honor always be made with "Formal and Impressive Ceremonial". The President further ordered that: "The recipient of a Medal of Honor will, whenever practicable, be ordered to Washington and the presentation will be made by the President".

NAVY MEDAL OF HONOR
(SECOND STYLE, 1913–1917)

Authorized on August 12, 1913. This was really a slight modification of the first style. The Secretary of the Navy issued an order changing the ribbon to light blue charged with thirteen white stars in order to standardize the ribbons of the Medal of Honor for both the Navy and the Army.

At the same time, the anchor suspension was simplified by removing the fouled lines from around it. The new regulations also specified that the medal would hereafter be worn "on a cravat, pendant from the neck."

On March 3, 1915, the award of the Navy Medal of Honor was opened to commissioned officers of the Navy and Marine Corps. Some of the awards were made retrospectively to cover service in prior conflicts as far back as the Spanish-American War.

NAVY MEDAL OF HONOR
(THIRD STYLE, 1917–1942)

Authorized by Congress on February 4, 1919. This "new" Medal of Honor was created for award to any person in the naval service who, while in action involving "actual conflict" with the enemy, distinguished himself conspicuously by gallantry and intrepidity at the risk of his life above and beyond the call of duty. At the same time, the "old" style Medal of Honor was retained for award to those who distinguished themselves by extraordinary heroism in the line of their profession – but not in direct action with an armed enemy.

Designed by the firm of Tiffany & Company of New York, this cross is often referred to as the "Tiffany Cross". It was the only time that the Navy used a different design for the Medal of Honor, and it was really designed to be awarded for service during World War 1, indicated by the inscription on the obverse of the medal, "United States Navy 1917–1918."

NAVY MEDAL OF HONOR
(FOURTH DESIGN, 1942–PRESENT)

An Act of Congress on August 7, 1942 established the Medal of Honor as a combat award only, abolished the "new" Medal of Honor of 1917–1918 and readopted the original design, the five-pointed inverted star, to be suspended by an anchor from a neck cravat and pad of light blue. The pad was charged with thirteen white stars. There have been some minor modifications to the ribbon and pad, but the medal adopted in 1942, as the highest award for gallantry the Navy bestows, is basically the same medal awarded to Navy and Marine Corps personnel now.

ARMY MEDAL OF HONOR
(FOURTH DESIGN, 1944–PRESENT)

This design, which is currently awarded, is simply the third type with a new neck ribbon. The color of the ribbon is the same light blue with the addition of a pad of pale blue containing thirteen white stars. The ribbon and pad have been modified slightly over the years, but the medal design has remained essentially the same.

This is the nation's highest award for gallantry, presented to members of the US Army who distinguish themselves conspicuously by gallantry and intrepidity at the risk of their lives above and beyond the call of duty while engaged in combat against an armed enemy of the United States.

The Army Medals of Honor were also given to members of the US Army Air Corps, for services during both World Wars and to members of the US Air Force during the Korean Conflict, before the creation of the Air Force Medal of Honor.

THE US AIR FORCE MEDAL OF HONOR

This was established by Congress on July 6, 1960, as the highest of several awards created specifically for the Air Force.

The medal is a five pointed star, each point tipped with trefoils and with a branch of laurel and oak in each arm. Centered in the star is a circle of thirty-four stars which surround the profile of the head from the Stature of Liberty. The star is surrounded by a green enameled laurel wreath.

NAVY MEDAL OF HONOR,
Fourth style (1942–Present)

ARMY MEDAL OF HONOR,
Fourth style (1944–Present)

THE US AIR FORCE MEDAL OF HONOR

The star is suspended from a trophy taken from the Air Force coat of arms. In the center is a baton with eagle claws at both ends, resting on a pair of aviator's wings with thunderbolts emitting from the center. This is attached to a horizontal bar with the word, "Valor".

The Air Force Medal of Honor is much larger than the other Medals, and a special large octagonal pad of light blue moiré with thirteen white stars was designed. This large pad is now also used for the smaller Army and Navy Medals of Honor, creating an unbalanced appearance.

■ THE 1917 REVIEW ■

Because the Medal of Honor was the only decoration that the Army had, some of the early acts which led to the awarding of the medal were deemed inappropriate in light of later events.

With the adoption of the "new" Medal of Honor, it was decided that further protection of the medal was necessary in light of the many awards — 2,625 — issued by this time. In order to strengthen the integrity of the medal, Section 122 of the National Defense Act of June 3, 1916, provided for establishing an Army board of review which would examine all awards and eliminate all those considered inappropriate.

After the total review of all cases, the board made its recommendations and on February 15, 1917, 911 names were struck from the list. These people were notified that their names were struck from the records, and they were requested to return the Medal of Honor that they had received. Incidentally, very few did return the medals.

CHAPTER EIGHT

THE BUILDING OF
THE PYRAMID OF HONOR

An Act of Congress on July 9, 1918 was the beginning of the whole system of decorations and awards that has become known as the "Pyramid of Honor". It was passed to protect the Medal of Honor, but at the same time recognized the need to create other awards.

The most far-reaching effect of this 1918 legislation was that for the first time in American history, it was established by law that there were degrees of service to the country, each worthy of recognition, and at the same time, clearly defined the type of deed necessary for the award of the medal.

DISTINGUISHED SERVICE CROSS,
Early award of the second style cross with the very large, obsolete Oak Leaves indicating an additional award.

It established the Distinguished Service Cross and the Army Distinguished Service Medal, and the "Silver Citation Star", (which would become the Silver Star Medal in 1932), each of them lower in precedence to the Medal of Honor, and abolished the Certificate of Merit for members of the Army. Further legislation by Congress on February 4, 1919 authorized the establishment of the similar awards for the Navy. The building of the Pyramid of Honor had begun.

In the beginning there were some problems: holders of the Certificate of Merit could exchange it for either the Distinguished Service Cross or the Distinguished Service Medal, and originally the Navy Cross ranked below the Distinguished Service Medal.

THE MARINE CORPS BREVET MEDAL
(OBSOLETE)

Authorized by Secretary of the Navy on June 7, 1921, this was awarded to all members of the Marine Corps holding Brevet Commissions for Bravery in action. These commissions were confirmed by the Senate in recognition of distinguished conduct and public service in the presence of the enemy.

This medal is one of the rarest US decorations, having been awarded retrospectively to only twenty-three officers for services during the Civil War, 1861–65; Spanish-American War, 1898; Philippine Insurrection, 1899–1913; and The Boxer Rebellion in China, 1900–1901.

THE CERTIFICATE OF MERIT
(OBSOLETE)

Established on March 3, 1847, during the Mexican War, this was originally created as a Certificate only, and during its lifetime there were only 1,206 Certificates awarded, most of these (539) for actions during the Mexican War.

On January 11, 1905, a medal was authorized to be

CERTIFICATE OF MERIT

DISTINGUISHED SERVICE CROSS

MARINE CORPS BREVET MEDAL

THE NAVY CROSS

THE AIR FORCE CROSS

**DEFENSE DISTINGUISHED
SERVICE MEDAL**

**ARMY DISTINGUISHED
SERVICE MEDAL**

**NAVY DISTINGUISHED
SERVICE MEDAL**

COAST GUARD DISTINGUISHED SERVICE MEDAL

AIR FORCE DISTINGUISHED SERVICE MEDAL

worn by all holders of the Certificate of Merit and to be awarded thereafter to any private soldier or noncommissioned officer . . . "who shall distinguish himself by Merit and Courage" and whom the President deemed worthy of the award.

Designed by Francis D. Millet, on the obverse is a bald eagle, much like a Roman war eagle standing on a baton, encircling an inscription. The reverse has the words "For Merit" and "United States Army" with a oak wreath and thirteen stars.

The medal was made obsolete on July 9, 1918, with the establishment of the Distinguished Service Cross and Distinguished Service Medal.

DISTINGUISHED SERVICE CROSS

Authorized on July 9, 1918 as an award for members of the Armed Forces of the United States who, while serving in any capacity with the US Army, distinguish themselves by extraordinary heroism not justifying the award of the Medal of Honor.

The current design is really the second design approved. The first style cross had the arms of the cross heavily ornamented with oak leaves, which detracted from the classic arms of the cross.

THE NAVY CROSS

Authorized on February 4, 1919 and awarded to officers and enlisted personnel of the US Navy and Marine Corps who distinguish themselves by extraordinary heroism not justifying the award of the Medal of Honor in military operations against an armed enemy. Originally awarded for combat heroism and other distinguished service, it was the Navy's third highest award.

An Act of Congress on August 7, 1942 gave the Navy Cross precedence over the Distinguished Service Medal, making it a combat decoration only, awarded only for extraordinary heroism in the presence of great danger and personal risk. It is now the second highest decoration for US Naval personnel.

THE AIR FORCE CROSS

Authorized on July 6, 1960, this decoration is the Air Force equivalent of the Distinguished Service Cross which the Air Force had continued to award to its personnel when it became a separate service branch.

DEFENSE DISTINGUISHED SERVICE MEDAL

Established on July 9, 1970, and awarded by the Secretary

of Defense to high ranking military officers, who perform exceptionally meritorious service in a degree of great responsibility with the Office of the Secretary of Defense, The Joint Chiefs of Staff, special or outstanding command in a Defense Agency or for any other Joint Activities designated by the Secretary of Defense.

■ DISTINGUISHED SERVICE ■ MEDALS

The separate service branches continue to award their respective Distinguished Service Medals to senior military officers of other services — even though the Defense Distinguished Service Medal was created in order to eliminate this practice.

ARMY DISTINGUISHED SERVICE MEDAL

Authorized on July 9, 1918, the medal is awarded to any member of the United States Armed Forces who, while

NAVY DISTINGUISHED SERVICE MEDAL,
First style designed by James E. Fraser, who was a member of the Commission on Fine Arts which had the responsibility of selecting the design of the medal. One hundred of these medals were made by the firm of Whitehead and Hoag, they were considered unsatisfactory by the Navy and this design was withdrawn, and the medal designed by Paul Manship was accepted and approved. This decoration was never issued, though a number have been found engraved.

THE SILVER STAR

**THE DEFENSE
SUPERIOR SERVICE MEDAL**

THE LEGION OF MERIT,
as awarded to U.S.
personnel for outstanding
Meritorious conduct in
combat, indicated by the
combat "V" for valor
devise on the ribbon.

serving in any capacity with the US Army after April 6, 1917, distinguishes themselves by exceptionally meritorious service to the government in a duty of great responsibility. It is awarded for both combat and noncombat service.

NAVY DISTINGUISHED SERVICE MEDAL

Authorized on February 4, 1919, and amended on August 7, 1942. The medal is awarded to any member of the Armed Forces who, while serving with the United States Navy in any capacity, since April 6, 1917, distinguishes themselves by exceptionally meritorious service to the government in a duty of great responsibility. Awarded for combat or noncombat services.

AIR FORCE DISTINGUISHED SERVICE MEDAL

Authorized on July 6, 1960. Awarded to any member of the Armed Forces who, while serving with the United States Air Force in any capacity distinguishes themselves by exceptionally meritorious service to the government in

a duty of great responsibility. The decoration may be awarded for combat and noncombat services.

COAST GUARD DISTINGUISHED SERVICE MEDAL

Although authorized on August 4, 1949, the design of this medal was not approved until February 1, 1961. Awarded to any person who, while serving in any capacity with the United States Coast Guard who distinguishes themselves by exceptionally meritorious service to the United States in a duty of great responsibility.

THE SILVER STAR

Authorized on July 9, 1918 as the "citation star" of the US Army, it was redesignated as a medal on August 8, 1932. The small silver citation star was placed in the center of a larger gilt star-shaped pendant, and a ribbon was added.

The star is awarded to any member of the United States Armed Forces who while serving in any capacity

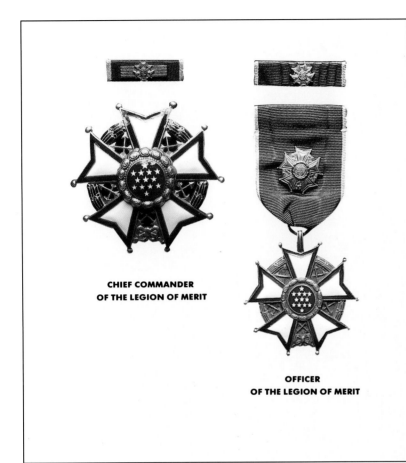

**CHIEF COMMANDER
OF THE LEGION OF MERIT**

**OFFICER
OF THE LEGION OF MERIT**

**COMMANDER OF THE
LEGION OF MERIT**

distinguished themselves by gallantry in action against an enemy of the United States or while serving with friendly forces against an opposing armed enemy force.

When the medal was created in 1932 it was made retrospective, so that those cited for gallantry as far back as the Spanish-American War of 1898, were eligible to receive the Silver Star. It is awarded for combat action only, and ranks as the third highest valor decoration of the United States.

■ DECORATIONS OF THE ■ DEPARTMENT OF DEFENSE

The first decoration specifically designed and awarded to members of joint service organizations and operations was the Joint Service Commendation Medal authorized in 1963. This was followed in 1970 with the creation of the Defense Distinguished Service Medal, in 1976, by the Defense Superior Service Medal, in 1977 by the Defense Meritorious Service Medal and in 1983 by the Joint Service Achievement Medal.

▨ THE DEFENSE SUPERIOR SERVICE MEDAL ▨

Established on February 6, 1976. Awarded by the Secretary of Defense to military officers who perform exceptionally meritorious service in a degree of great responsibility with the Office of the Secretary of Defense, the Joint Chiefs of Staff, special or outstanding command in a defense agency or any other joint activity designated by the Secretary. The services rendered will be similar to those required for the award of the Legion of Merit.

▨ THE LEGION OF MERIT ▨

Authorized on July 20, 1942, and amended on March 15, 1955, this was the first United States decoration created specifically as an award for citizens of other nations, and it is the first award to have different "degrees" to conform with the decorations of other nations.

It is awarded to members of the United Nations Armed Forces for exceptionally meritorious conduct in the performance of outstanding service to the United States. Originally awarded to both officers and enlisted men, the

Legion of Merit has been continuously upgraded since its inception. Currently the recipient must occupy a position of great responsibility and would normally be a high ranking officer of staff or flag rank.

The different degrees of the Legion of Merit are:

CHIEF COMMANDER OF THE LEGION OF MERIT

Awarded to chiefs of state or heads of government. It is a large star of the order worn on the breast.

COMMANDER OF THE LEGION OF MERIT

Awarded to foreign recipients who are equivalent to a chief of staff in the United States, or to a leader lower than the head of state. It is a large badge of the order worn round the neck.

OFFICER OF THE LEGION OF MERIT

Awarded to foreign generals or admirals, high ranking civil authorities and foreign attachés. This is a breast decoration with a miniature of the medal worn on the suspension ribbon.

LEGION OF MERIT, LEGIONNAIRE

This degree is awarded to all other eligible personnel.

DISTINGUISHED FLYING CROSS

Authorized on July 2, 1926, and amended January 8, 1938. The Distinguished Flying Cross is awarded to any officer and enlisted member of the United States Armed Forces who shall distinguish themselves by herosim or extraordinary achievement while participating in an aerial flight, subsequent to November 11, 1918.

The first award was made to Captain Charles A. Lindbergh, for his solo flight across the Atlantic. Order recipients include Commander Richard E. Byrd, for his historic flight over the North Pole and aviatrix Amelia Earhart.

■ NON-COMBAT AWARDS ■

The following decorations are awarded for heroism, usually enacted at voluntary risk of life, but not involving actual combat. Most of these decorations are presented for outstanding heroism in the saving of lives, and are commonly called the "Military Lifesaving Medals."

THE SOLDIER'S MEDAL

Authorized by an Act of Congress on July 2, 1926, and awarded to any person who, while serving in any capacity with the United States Army, National Guard or Organized Reserves shall distinguish himself or herself by "Heroism not involving actual conflict with an armed enemy." The act of Heroism must have meant personal hazard or danger and the voluntary risk of the recipient's life.

NAVY AND MARINE CORPS MEDAL

Authorized on August 7, 1942, the day Marines landed on Guadalcanal in the Solomon Islands. This Medal is awarded to anyone serving with the Navy or Marine Corps, including Reserves, who since December 6, 1941, shall distinguish themselves by heroism not involving actual conflict with the enemy.

A future President of the United States, John F. Kennedy was awarded the Navy and Marine Corps Medal for heroism, while serving as a junior Naval officer in the Pacific during World War II. The complete story of his act of heroism was documented in a very fine book and movie, titled *PT-109*.

AIRMAN'S MEDAL

Authorized on July 6, 1960, the Airman's Medal is awarded to any member of the United States Air Force, or other Armed Forces serving in any capacity with the Air Force, who shall distinguish himself or herself by a heroic act, usually at the voluntary risk of his or her life but not involving actual combat.

During time of war, the United States Coast Guard serves as part of the Navy, and is eligible for all of the decorations and awards of the Naval service. The only Medal of Honor awarded to a member of the Coast Guard was posthumously awarded to Signalman First Class Douglas Albert Munro, USCG, during the Guadalcanal campaign. The Medal now rests in Munro Hall, at the Coast Guard Academy, in New London, Connecticut.

COAST GUARD MEDAL

Authorized in 1951, although the medal was not struck until 1958. It is awarded to any person serving in any capacity with the Coast Guard who shall distinguish himself by heroism not involving actual conflict with the enemy. The individual must have performed a voluntary act of courage surpassing normal expectation and in the face of great danger. For an act of lifesaving, the individual must have displayed heroism at the risk of his life.

LEGION OF MERIT, LEGIONNAIRE   DISTINGUISHED FLYING CROSS   SOLDIER'S MEDAL

NAVY AND MARINE CORPS MEDAL

AIRMAN'S MEDAL   COAST GUARD MEDAL

BRONZE STAR

PURPLE HEART

GOLD LIFESAVING MEDAL,
First Class (Obverse)

SILVER LIFESAVING MEDAL,
Second Class (Obverse)

GOLD LIFESAVING MEDAL,
(1882–1949)

SILVER LIFESAVING MEDAL,
(1882–1949)

GOLD LIFESAVING MEDAL,
(1949–Present)

THE BRONZE STAR

(ALL SERVICES)

Authorized on February 4, 1944, this is awarded to any person in any branch of the military service who, while serving in any capacity with the armed forces of the United States on or after December 7, 1941, who shall distinguish himself by heroic or meritorious achievement or service, (although not for aerial flight).

THE PURPLE HEART

Authorized in 1932, this is the modern form of the original Purple Heart established by General George Washington in 1782. It is awarded for combat action only and is awarded to any person wounded in action while serving with the armed forces of the United States. It is also awarded posthumously to next of kin of personnel killed in action, or who died of wounds received in action after April 5, 1917.

Originally one of the lesser decorations in the Pyramid of Honor, it was elevated to its current position by President Ronald Reagan in 1985. Designed by Elizabeth Will, this heart-shaped medal is one of the best known and

most beautiful of all US decorations. The decoration includes a fine profile of Washington, as well as the Washington family coat of arms at the top of the heart.

■ MEDALS FOR LIFESAVING ■

The original Lifesaving medals, created on June 20, 1874 were not made to be worn. The Gold Medal had the inscription, "Life Saving Medal of the First Class", and the Silver, the inscription, "Life Saving Medal of the Second Class" at the top.

An Act of Congress dated June 18, 1878, made changes in the original designs of both medals, omitting the wording, and making them slightly smaller. These medals are commonly called the "Original Life Saving Medals".

GOLD LIFE SAVING MEDAL, 1882–1949

Authorized by an Act of Congress, May 4, 1882. This award is a modification of the original medal and is awarded to any person who rescues or endeavors to rescue any other person from drowning, shipwreck, or

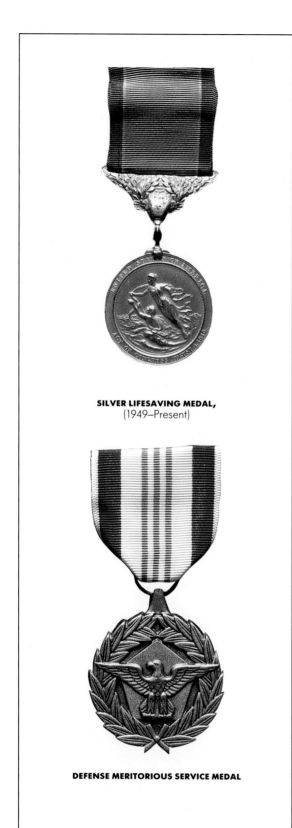

SILVER LIFESAVING MEDAL,
(1949–Present)

DEFENSE MERITORIOUS SERVICE MEDAL

other peril of the water. The rescue must take place in waters within the United States or subject to its jurisdiction, or one of the parties must be a citizen of the United States, and the rescue or attempted rescue must have been made at the risk of the rescuer's own life, with evidence of extreme and heroic daring. The medal is worn on a ruby red ribbon.

GOLD LIFE SAVING MEDAL, 1949–PRESENT

The current medal changes started with a memorandum on March 13, 1946 from Admiral J.F. Farley, who was then Commandant of the Coast Guard. Several changes were suggested, including changing the color of the ribbons of the medals and recommending that the size of the medals be reduced to enable them to ". . . present a more harmonious appearance when they are worn on the uniform with other medals . . ."

The revised medal was struck in pure gold. The inscription on the lower obverse was changed to: "Act of Congress August 4, 1949", and the new gold, red and white ribbon was adopted.

THE SILVER LIFESAVING MEDAL, 1882–1949

The Silver Lifesaving Medal is awarded under the same conditions as the Gold Lifesaving Medal, except that the act need not involve the degree of heroism and risk called for in the case of the Gold Lifesaving Medal.

THE SILVER LIFESAVING MEDAL, 1949–PRESENT

The Act of Congress on August 4, 1949 that changed and modified the Gold Lifesaving Medal also changed the Silver Lifesaving Medal. The design remained the same, but the medal and eagle suspension bar were reduced in size, and the inscription on the obverse was changed. The current ribbon suspension was also adopted.

The Lifesaving medals have very decorative additional award bars composed of the same medal as the medal previously awarded the recipient.

DEPARTMENT OF DEFENSE MERITORIOUS SERVICE MEDAL

Established by Executive Order 12019 on November 3, 1977, the Defense Meritorious Service Medal is awarded to military personnel serving with or assigned to a number

THE AIR MEDAL

MERITORIOUS SERVICE MEDAL

**JOINT SERVICE
COMMENDATION MEDAL**

**ARMY
COMMENDATION MEDAL**

**NAVY
COMMENDATION MEDAL**

**AIR FORCE
COMMENDATION MEDAL**

of joint activities including The Secretary of Defense, Organizations of the Joint Chiefs of Staff and Headquarters of Joint Commands, and other joint activities and specified commands that may be designated by the Secretary of Defense.

The medal is awarded for non-combat meritorious achievement or service that is incontestably exceptional and of a magnitude that clearly places the individual above his peers while serving in one of the assignments designated.

THE MERITORIOUS SERVICE MEDAL

Authorized on January 16, 1969, and awarded to any member of the Armed Forces of the United States who distinguishes himself or herself by either outstanding achievement or meritorious service to the United States. It was established as a junior award of the Legion of Merit and to replace the Bronze Star for the recognition of meritorious non-combat services.

AIR MEDAL

Established on May 11, 1942. The Air Medal is awarded to any member of the Armed Forces of the United States who subsequent to September 8, 1939, shall have distinguished himself by meritorious achievement while participating in aerial flight. It was given for combat or non-combat action, and conferred in recognition of single acts of heroism or merit for operational activities against an armed enemy. Additionally, it is given for meritorious services, or for sustained distinction in the performance of duties involving regular and frequent participation in aerial flight.

■ COMMENDATION AND ■ ACHIEVEMENTS MEDALS

Each of the military services created Commendation Medals and Achievement Medals of their respective branches, and each of these branches could also award these medals to members of the other services. These decorations could be awarded for combat and non-combat actions and services, and are similar in design.

JOINT SERVICE COMMENDATION MEDAL

Established on June 25, 1963. Awarded by the Secretary of Defense, the Joint Chiefs of Staff, and other Depart-

COAST GUARD COMMENDATION MEDAL,
First style, (1951–1968)

COAST GUARD COMMENDATION MEDAL,
Current style

ment of Defense agencies or joint activities to members of the Armed Forces who distinguish themselves by meritorious achievement or service after January 1, 1965. Members of all the services are eligible.

ARMY COMMENDATION MEDAL

Authorized in 1945. Awarded to members of the Armed Forces who, while serving in any capacity with the Army on or after December 7, 1941, shall distinguish themselves, either in combat or non-combat action, by meritorious achievement or meritorious service.

NAVY COMMENDATION MEDAL

Authorized on January 11, 1944. Originally created as a ribbon called the Navy Commendation Ribbon, it was the first of the commendation awards. Awarded to members of the Navy and Marine Corps, or other members of the Armed Forces serving with these branches, who distinguish themselves by heroism, outstanding achievement or meritorious service. This is a personal decoration, which has often been awarded for Life Saving, in place of the medals originally created for this purpose.

AIR FORCE COMMENDATION MEDAL

Authorized on March 28, 1958. Awarded to officers and enlisted men of the Air Force, and other members of the Armed Forces of the United States who, while serving with the Air Force after March 24, 1958, shall distinguish themselves by meritorious achievement and service.

Designed by the Institute of Heraldry, this decoration, like the other Commendation medals, is a bronze hexagon shape. On the obverse is the seal of the Air Force.

COAST GUARD
COMMENDATION MEDAL
(FIRST TYPE 1951–1968)

Authorized by the Secretary of the Treasury on August 26, 1947 In its original form it was only a ribbon bar – the medal pendant was not created until July 5, 1951. On October 2, 1959, it was re-designated as the Coast Guard Commendation Medal. Awarded to members of the US Coast Guard, Coast Guard Reserves and to other members of the US Armed Forces, serving in any capacity with the Coast Guard, for heroism, or meritorious service resulting in unusual and outstanding achievement rendered while the Coast Guard is under the jurisdiction of the Treasury Department.

JOINT SERVICE ACHIEVEMENT MEDAL

NAVY ACHIEVEMENT MEDAL

**ARMY
ACHIEVEMENT MEDAL**

**AIR FORCE
ACHIEVEMENT MEDAL**

**COAST GUARD
ACHIEVEMENT MEDAL**

COAST GUARD COMMENDATION MEDAL
(SECOND TYPE, 1968–PRESENT)

The second design of this medal was approved by the Commandant of the Coast Guard on June 11, 1968.

Awarded to Members of the US Coast Guard, Coast Guard Reserve and to other members of the United States Armed Forces serving in any capacity with the Coast Guard, who distinguish themselves by heroism, outstanding achievement or meritorious service above that normally expected and worthy of special recognition.

THE JOINT SERVICE ACHIEVEMENT MEDAL

The Achievement Medals were created by the Armed Forces as a junior award to their Commendation Medals. The citations are similar but the services are usually considered of a lesser degree than that required for the Commendation Medals.
Established by the Secretary of Defense on August 3, 1983, and awarded in the name of the Secretary of Defense for either outstanding achievement or meritorious service. It takes precedence over the Achievement Medals of the Military Services.

NAVY ACHIEVEMENT MEDAL

Authorized by the Secretary of the Navy on January 24, 1962, and awarded to junior officers and enlisted personnel serving in any capacity with the Navy and Marine Corps who distinguish themselves by outstanding professional achievement or for leadership. Originally a non-combat award, the achievement medal is now awarded for both combat and non-combat service. The combat "V" device is worn on the ribbon if stipulated in the citation.

ARMY ACHIEVEMENT MEDAL

Authorized on April 10, 1981. Awarded to members of the Armed Forces who, while serving in any capacity with the Army in a non-combat area on or after August 1, 1981, shall distinguish themselves by outstanding achievement or by meritorious service.

AIR FORCE ACHIEVEMENT MEDAL

Authorized on April 20, 1980. Awarded to Air Force personnel for outstanding achievement or meritorious service rendered specifically on behalf of the Air Force. It may also be awarded for acts of heroism.

THE COAST GUARD ACHIEVEMENT MEDAL

Established as the Secretary of the Treasury Commendation for Achievement Award on January 29, 1964, this award was subsequently designated as the Secretary of Transportation Commendation Award on March 13, 1967. This was designated as the Coast Guard Achievement Medal on June 11, 1968.

It is awarded to all members of the Coast Guard, including reserves, and members of other branches of the Armed Forces when serving with Coast Guard units for outstanding leadership, professional achievement and superior performance of duty in either peacetime or combat situations.

COMBAT ACTION RIBBON

Authorized on February 17, 1969, this ribbon is awarded to members of the Navy, Marine Corps and Coast Guard for combat action service. The principal requirement is that the personnel must have been in a ground or surface combat fire fight or action during which they were under enemy fire and that their performance under fire must have been satisfactory.

OUTSTANDING AIRMAN OF THE YEAR RIBBON

Authorized on February 21, 1968. It is awarded to enlisted service members of the US Air Force who are nominated by their respective major commands and separate operating agencies for competition in the Outstanding Airmen

of the Year Programs. The award of this ribbon was made retrospective to June 1960.

AIR FORCE RECOGNITION RIBBON

Authorized by the Chief of Staff, US Air Force on October 12, 1980. It is awarded to named individual Air Force recipients of special trophies and awards as outlined in US Air Force regulations; this does not include the 12 Outstanding Airmen of the Year nominees. Bronze oak-leaf clusters for subsequent awards are authorized to be worn on this ribbon.

AIR FORCE LONGEVITY SERVICE AWARD

Authorized on November 25, 1957. Awarded to all active service members of the US Air Force who complete four years of honorable active or reserve service with any branch of the United States Armed Forces. This ribbon award replaces the Federal Service Stripes that were previously worn on the uniform. Subsequent periods of service are denoted by a bronze oak-leaf cluster.

AIR FORCE COMBAT READINESS MEDAL

Authorized on March 9, 1964, and amended August 28, 1967, this was originally created as a personal decoration ranking above the Commendation Medals, but is now an achievement/service medal. It is awarded to members of the US Air Force and Air Force Reserve, and to members of other services after August 1, 1960, for sustained (usually three years) individual combat or mission readiness or preparedness for direct weapon-system employment.

CHAPTER NINE

UNIT CITATIONS AND UNIT AWARDS

U nit awards are made to entire organizations for outstanding heroism or achievement. They are not presented as a means of recognizing single, individual actions, but to cite the combined efforts of every member of an organization in the accomplishment of a common goal.

Unit citations and awards are indicated by ribbon bars only, there are no medal attachments involved. When military personnel are wearing decorations and medals in full dress, these ribbon bars are worn separately on the right breast.

The need for such an award became important with the entry of the United States in World War II, and the first unit award was the Presidential Unit Citation of the Navy created by President Roosevelt in 1942.

PRESIDENTIAL UNIT CITATION
(ARMY AND AIR FORCE)

This was created by Executive Order 9075 on February 26, 1942, as the Distinguished Unit Citation and superseded by Executive Order 10694, on January 10, 1957 which re-designated it as the Presidential Unit Citation. It is conferred on units of the US Armed Forces for extraordinary heroism in action against an armed enemy on or after December 7, 1941. The unit must display such gallantry, determination, and esprit de corps in accomplishing its mission as to set it apart from and above other units participating in the same campaign.

PRESIDENTIAL UNIT CITATION
(NAVY AND MARINE CORPS)

Authorized by Executive Order 9050 on February 6, 1942,

this is awarded by the Secretary of the Navy in the name of the President, to any ship, aircraft, or naval unit, or any Marine Corps aircraft, detachment, or higher unit for outstanding performance in action against an armed enemy of the United States on or after December 7, 1941.

Though created as a combat award, there have been two non-combat awards authorized. For the *USS Nautilus* (SSN 571) for the first cruise of a nuclear submarine, July 22 to August 5, 1958, and to the *USS Triton* (SSN 586) for the submerged circumnavigation of the world, February 16 to May 10, 1960.

VALOROUS UNIT AWARD
(ARMY)

This is awarded by the Army to Units for extraordinary heroism against an armed enemy in actions on or after August 3, 1963. It is awarded for a lesser degree of gallantry, determination and esprit de corps than that required for the Presidential Unit citation. The degree of gallantry must be the same as that for an individual to earn the Silver Star Medal.

NAVY UNIT COMMENDATION

Established by the Secretary of the Navy on December 18, 1944 and awarded by the Secretary with the approval of the President, this Unit commendation is conferred on any ship, aircraft, detachment, or other unit of the US Navy or Marine Corps which, subsequent to December 6,

1941, distinguished itself by outstanding heroism in action against the enemy, but not sufficient to warrant award of the Presidential Unit Citation.

It is also awarded for extremely meritorious service not involving combat but in support of military operations which were outstanding when compared to other units performing similar services.

COAST GUARD UNIT COMMENDATION

Authorized by the Commandant of the Coast Guard effective January 1, 1963, this is awarded by the Commandant of the Coast Guard to any ship, aircraft, or any other Coast Guard unit which distinguished itself by valorous or extremely meritorious service in support of US Coast Guard operations.

AIR FORCE OUTSTANDING UNIT AWARD

Authorized by Department of the Air Force General Order 1, on January 6, 1954. This is awarded by the Secretary of the Air Force to units which have distinguished themselves by exceptionally meritorious service or outstanding achievement that sets it above and apart from similar units.

AIR FORCE ORGANIZATIONAL EXCELLENCE AWARD

Authorized by the Secretary of the Air Force on August 26, 1969, this is awarded to recognize the achievements and accomplishments of US Air Force organizations or activities (usually small, unique and unnumbered groups) that do not meet the requirements for the Air Force Outstanding Unit Award.

JOINT MERITORIOUS UNIT AWARD

Authorized by the Secretary of Defense on June 10, 1981, this award was originally called the Department of Defense Meritorious Unit Award. It is awarded in the name of the Secretary of Defense to joint activities (all services) for meritorious achievement or service, superior to that which is normally expected, for actions in the following situations: combat with an armed enemy of the United States, or during a declared national emergency, or under extraordinary circumstances that involve national interests.

ARMY MERITORIOUS UNIT COMMENDATION

Awarded by the Department of the Army to units for exceptionally meritorious conduct in performance of outstanding service for at least six continuous months during military operations against an armed enemy on or after January 1, 1944. Service in a combat zone is not required, but the service must be directly related to the combat effort. This replaces the Combat Infantryman's Badge as a unit award.

NAVY MERITORIOUS UNIT COMMENDATION

Authorized by SECNAVNOTE (Secretary of the Navy Note) 1650, on July 17, 1967, and awarded by the Secretary to any unit of the US Navy or Marine Corps which distinguished itself, by either valorous or meritorious achievement considered outstanding when compared to other units performing similar service, but not sufficient to justify award of the Navy Unit Commendation. Awarded for combat or non-combat services.

COAST GUARD MERITORIOUS UNIT COMMENDATION

Authorized by the Commandant, US Coast Guard on November 13, 1973, it is awarded by the Commandant to any unit of the US Coast Guard or Coast Guard Reserve which has distinguished itself by either valorous or meritorious achievement or service in support of US Coast Guard operations. The Operational Distinguishing Device (silver letter "O") may be worn on this ribbon when authorized.

NAVY "E" AWARD RIBBON

A Secretary of the Navy Recommendation in June of 1976 established this award to replace the Battle Efficiency Award (the letter "E") which had been worn sewn to the sleeve of the uniform. It is authorized to be worn by all crew members of ships and aviation squadrons winning the fleet-wide eighteen month competitive cycle which has exercises testing all phases of battle readiness. The Battle Efficiency Award, sometimes called the Navy "E" Award, consisted of the above mentioned cloth insignia and a battle pennant to be displayed by the ship or unit winning the award.

■ ARMED FORCES ■
GOOD CONDUCT MEDALS

The following awards were created by the various branches of the Armed Forces to recognize the continuous good conduct and outstanding service in their particular branch of service.

They are awarded for active duty service of a credible, above average service, noted by obedience, sobriety, military efficiency and behavior, leadership, military appearance and intelligence. These medals have undergone subtle changes in design and time requirements since their inception.

The first of the awards was the Navy Good Conduct Badge, created by the Secretary of the Navy on April 26, 1869. This particular badge was used until 1884.

NAVY GOOD CONDUCT BADGE

(FIRST TYPE 1869–1884)

Authorized on April 26, 1869, and awarded to any man holding a Continuous Service Certificate who has distinguished himself for obedience, sobriety and cleanliness, and who was proficient in seamanship and gunnery, upon the expiration of his enlistment. Any person receiving three badges was given the rating of petty officer, and could not be reduced in rank except by sentence of a court martial.

The badge is a Maltese cross of nickel silver, with a

circular medallion with a rope border in the center with the words, "Fidelity Zeal Obedience" and "U.S.N."

ARMY GOOD CONDUCT MEDAL

Authorized on June 28, 1941 and amended on April 10, 1953. Awarded on a selective basis to enlisted members of the Regular US Army who distinguished themselves by exemplary behavior, efficiency and fidelity throughout a specified period of continuous enlisted service. Although usually awarded for three years service, this was reduced to one year during wartime service. Clasps are awarded for second and subsequent awards.

NAVY GOOD CONDUCT MEDAL

Authorized on November 21, 1884, and awarded on a selective basis to enlisted service members of the United States Navy, and US Navy Reserve (active duty) for four years of continuous active service of a creditable above-

NAVY GOOD CONDUCT MEDAL,
Early versions had additional awards indicated by rope-bordered bars, that had the name of the ship or duty station engraved on them, and the reverse was engraved with recipient's Continuous Service Certificate Number, and the dates of service.

**NAVY GOOD CONDUCT
MEDAL**

**ARMY GOOD CONDUCT
MEDAL**

**NAVY GOOD CONDUCT
BADGE,**
First style (1869–1884)

**MARINE CORPS GOOD
CONDUCT MEDAL**

**AIR FORCE GOOD CONDUCT
MEDAL**

**COAST GUARD GOOD
CONDUCT MEDAL**

**COAST GUARD GOOD
CONDUCT MEDAL,**
Original style

**ARMY RESERVE
COMPONENTS
ACHIEVEMENT MEDAL**

**NAVAL RESERVE
MERITORIOUS SERVICE
MEDAL**

**ORGANIZED MARINE CORPS
RESERVE MEDAL**

**ORGANIZED MARINE CORPS
RESERVE MEDAL**
(First style, obverse)

**AIR RESERVE FORCES
MERITORIOUS SERVICE
AWARD**

average nature in the areas of professional performance, military behavior, leadership, military appearance and adaptability.

MARINE CORPS GOOD CONDUCT MEDAL

Authorized on July 20, 1896, this award has had many amendments. Since July 9, 1953 it is awarded to enlisted personnel of the US Marine Corps, Regular or Reserve, for obedience, sobriety, neatness, bearing and intelligence during three years of continuous active service.

AIR FORCE GOOD CONDUCT MEDAL

Authorized on July 6, 1960, (when all of the Air Force medals were created), although the medals were not issued until 1963. Awarded to enlisted service members of the US Air Force for exemplary conduct during a three-year period of active service, (reduced to one year's service during a time of war). Personnel awarded this medal must have had character and efficiency ratings of excellent or higher throughout the qualifying period.

COAST GUARD GOOD CONDUCT MEDAL

Authorized on May 18, 1921, and awarded on a selective basis to enlisted personnel of the Coast Guard and Coast Guard Reserve for periods of three year's continuous service above the average. Recipients must have been recommended by their commanding officer for proficiency in rating, sobriety, obedience, industry, courage and neatness throughout the period of service.

The original medal was about 20 percent larger than the present award, and had a top suspension bar with the words, "U.S. Coast Guard". Additional awards were indicated by a wide clasp with the name of the ship or station engraved upon it, but this has been replaced with a star for additional awards.

ARMY RESERVE COMPONENTS ACHIEVEMENT MEDAL

Authorized on October 30, 1971, the medal is awarded for exemplary behavior, efficiency and fidelity while serving as a member of the US Army National Guard or Reserve Troop Program Unit.

It is usually awarded for a period of four years service with either organization. Subsequent awards are indicated by an oak-leaf cluster worn on the ribbon.

NAVAL RESERVE MERITORIOUS SERVICE MEDAL

Authorized on September 12, 1959, originally as a ribbon bar only. The ribbon was replaced by the medal on June 22, 1962. It is awarded on a selective basis to US Navy Reservists who fulfill with distinction the obligations of inactive Reservists, meeting certain attendance and performance requirements at a higher level than that normally expected.

Following the lead of the Navy, the Coast Guard created a similar award, originally as a ribbon called the Coast Guard Reserve Meritorious Service Ribbon, which has since been replaced by the Coast Guard Reserve Good Conduct Medal.

ORGANIZED MARINE CORPS RESERVE MEDAL

Authorized on February 19, 1939, and awarded to officers and enlisted personnel of the US Marine Corps Reserve who, subsequent to July 1, 1925, have fulfilled certain designated military service requirements within a four year period of service in the Organized Marine Corps Reserve. (This medal was originally awarded for service only in the Fleet Marine Corps Reserve. The first medals issued had the words "Fleet Marine Corps Reserve" on the obverse of the medal, and are quite rare).

AIR RESERVE FORCES MERITORIOUS SERVICE AWARD

Authorized as a ribbon bar on April 1, 1964, it was changed to a medal on May 1, 1973. Awarded for exemplary behavior, efficiency, and fidelity during a four year period while serving in an enlisted status in the US Air Reserve Forces, (Air Force Reserve).

MARINE CORPS RESERVE RIBBON

Authorized on December 17, 1945 and awarded to members of the US Marine Corps Reserve for each ten year period of honorable service in the Marine Corps Reserve between December 17, 1945 and December 17, 1965. Military service after the later date shall only be credited toward the Armed Forces Reserve Medal.

COAST GUARD RESERVE GOOD CONDUCT MEDAL

Initially established as the Coast Guard Reserve Meritorious Service ribbon, this award was renamed and authorized as the Coast Guard Reserve Good Conduct Medal on September 3, 1981.

**COAST GUARD RESERVE
GOOD CONDUCT MEDAL**

**ARMED FORCES RESERVE
MEDAL,**
Obverse for all services

**THE PRISONER OF WAR
MEDAL**

Awarded on a selective basis to Coast Guard enlisted Reservists on inactive duty who fulfill with distinction the obligations of inactive Reservists. The service required is similar to that required for the Coast Guard Good Conduct Medal for active duty personnel of the Coast Guard.

NAVAL RESERVE MEDAL 1938–1958

Authorized on September 12, 1938, and awarded to officers and enlisted men for each ten year period of honorable military service in the Naval Reserve prior to September 12, 1958. After the establishment of the Armed Forces Reserve Medal in 1950, a member of the Naval Reserve who would be eligible for either award could choose which he would receive.

ARMED FORCES RESERVE MEDAL

Created to replace the long service and good conduct medals awarded to the different branches of the Armed Forces of the United States, and authorized on September 25, 1950 and amended on March 19, 1953. It is awarded to any service member or former service member of the Reserve Components of the Armed Forces of the United States who completes or has completed a total of ten year's of honorable and satisfactory military service, in one or more Reserve components of the United States Armed Forces.

Designed by the Institute of Heraldry, the obverse of the medal is the same for all services, and there are six different reverse designs showing the emblem for each service and the inscription, "Armed Forces Reserve".

THE PRISONER OF WAR MEDAL

Authorized by Congress, and signed into law by President Ronald Reagan in 1986. Awarded to any member of the United States Armed Forces who was a prisoner of war after April 5, 1917 (the date of America's entry in World War I), and to any person who was taken prisoner or held captive while engaged in action against an enemy of the United States, or while serving with friendly forces engaged in armed conflict. The recipient's conduct, while in captivity, must have been honorable. The medal can be received posthumously by the next of kin of the recipient.

CHAPTER TEN

CAMPAIGN MEDALS OF THE UNITED STATES 1861–1917

The major difference between decorations and campaign and service medals is that decorations are awarded for individual acts of gallantry, heroism and exceptional and meritorious services. They are usually designed in an unusual shape such as stars and crosses. Campaign and service medals are awarded to all personnel for serving in a particular war or campaign. Commemorative medals are usually round to distinguish them from individual decorations.

President Theodore Roosevelt must be considered as the creator of campaign medals of the United States. The President was always a great supporter of the military, and he questioned why there was no medal to indicate that men had served in campaigns and wars.

He was informed that efforts had been made for many years to induce the Congress to authorize the award of service medals, but without result. Never one to let red tape and the slow moving machinery of legislation deter him, he announced that campaign service medals were officially designated as badges, and he, as President and Commander-in-Chief of the army and navy, could designate badges of this kind to be worn on the uniform of the men who had participated in the respective campaigns.

Accordingly, such an order was promulgated, and announced by the Secretary of War in General Order 4, on January 11, 1905. This order created the Certificate of Merit badge, and the Army campaign badges for the Civil War, the Indian Wars, the Spanish-American War, the Philippine Insurrection and the China Relief Expedition of 1900–1901. This was amended on August 13, 1908 by General Order 129, which established the areas and time limits for each of these awards.

Awards for Navy and Marine Corps personnel followed with the creation of their distinctive medals by the Navy Department Special Order 81, issued on June 27, 1908. It is interesting that when these medals were created, each

of the services had their own distinctive medals. The ribbons were identical.

Prior to the creation of these campaign medals, the Navy had created Good Conduct badges for both the Navy and Marine Corps, and Congress had voted two commemorative medals, the Medal for the Battle of Manila Bay, commonly called the "Dewey Medal", and the West Indies Naval Campaign Medal, commonly called the "Sampson Medal".

■ THE CIVIL WAR, 1861–1865 ■

In December of 1860, after the election of Lincoln, and after forty years of political compromise between the states of the North and South, it was announced, "that the union . . . between South Carolina and other States under the name of the United States is hereby dissolved." By February, six other southern states had seceded, and on February 8th, these seven states formed a new union – the Confederate States of America. When Confederate batteries opened fire on Federal forces in Charleston harbor on April 12, 1861, there began a War that few on either side believed would be very long or costly. They were wrong.

For four long years this deeply divisive war, pitted father against son, brother against brother, and the North against the South. It finally ended on April 9, 1865, when General Lee surrendered to General Grant at Appomattox Court House.

After the War many veterans organizations and societies were formed which had medals as membership badges. The largest of thse, the GAR (Grand Army of the Republic) had hundreds of different badges. There were also Confederate Veteran Groups. Nevertheless, all these medals and badges, of either side, are unofficial.

The only official Federal medal awarded during the

CIVIL WAR MEDAL,
Army

CIVIL WAR MEDAL,
Army with original ribbon

War was the Medal of Honor. It was forty years before an official medal was issued specifically for service during the Civil War, to be awarded retrospectively.

CIVIL WAR MEDAL
(ARMY)

Authorized by the War Department in 1907, and awarded for service in the Regular or Volunteer Army or in the Militia in the service of the United States during the Civil War between April 15, 1861, and April 9, 1865, — or for service in Texas, to August 20, 1866.

Designed by Francis D. Millet, the obverse features a bust of Abraham Lincoln, with the legend, "With Malice Toward None, With Charity For All".

The original ribbon had a narrow white center stripe, flanked on either side by equal stripes of red, white and blue. This was changed in 1913 to half blue and half gray.

CIVIL WAR MEDAL
(NAVY AND MARINE CORPS)

Established on June 27, 1908 and awarded to officers and enlisted men who served in the Navy and Marine Corps during the Civil War, between April 15, 1861 and April 9, 1865.

It was designed by the firm of Bailey, Banks and Biddle. The obverse has a scene of the battle between the *Monitor* and *Merrimac*, and inscription, "The Civil War, 1861–1865."

■ THE INDIAN WARS, ■ 1865–1898

The United States Army became engaged in a series of expeditions, campaigns and small wars that lasted over thirty years. There were twelve distinct campaigns from 1865 to 1891 against some of the greatest Indian nations, such as the Cheyenne, Arapahoe, Kiowa, Comanche, Apache and Sioux. Smaller engagements continued up to 1898, varying from skirmishes to pitched battles.

Hardly a three-month period passed without some encounter, yet these Indian Wars went unnoticed for some time. It was not until March of 1890, that the Congress applied to Indian fighters the term "veterans" meaning soldiers who had participated in campaigns against an armed enemy of the United States. It was not for seventeen more years that a medal was authorized to indicate this service.

(ARMY)

Authorized by the War Department in 1907, and awarded for members of the army who served in any of twelve different major campaigns against hostile Indians from 1865 to 1891, and in such minor campaigns against hostiles as approved by the Army. On the obverse, a mounted Indian is shown wearing war bonnet and carrying a spear, plus the words, "Indian Wars", a buffalo skull and arrowheads.

The original ribbon of solid red with darker red edges was changed in 1917 to distinguish it from the French Legion of Honor, because many of the senior officers and soldiers of the US Army serving in France wore it.

THE SPANISH-AMERICAN WAR – 1898

The sinking of the US Battleship *Maine* in Havana Harbor, Cuba on February 15, 1898 led to the United States declaring war against Spain on April 11th. The conflict lasted only ten weeks, and was chiefly a naval contest with fighting in both the Atlantic and Pacific Oceans.

The War ended with a peace treaty, signed in Paris on December 10th. With this treaty Spain surrendered all claim to Cuba, Puerto Rico, the Philippine Islands, and Guam.

This so-called "Splendid little War" led to the decline of Spain and the emergence of the United States as a world power. It also produced three commemorative medals, four campaign and two occupation medals.

BATTLE OF MANILA BAY MEDAL

This was authorized by Resolution No. 38 of the Congress, on June 3, 1898. It was awarded to officers and men of the Navy and Marine Corps who were crew members of the ships of the Asiatic Squadron to commemorate their participation in the battle of Manila Bay on May 1, 1898. The names of the recipient and his ship were engraved on each medal before presentation.

The obverse features a bust of Admiral Dewey, the Commanding Officer hence its common name: the "Dewey Medal".

WEST INDIES NAVAL CAMPAIGN MEDAL, 1898

Authorized by Congressional Special Order 70, March 3, 1901. The Medal was awarded to officers and men of the

CIVIL WAR MEDAL,
Navy and Marine Corps

INDIAN WARS MEDAL,
Army

**BATTLE OF MANILA BAY
MEDAL,**
(Dewey Medal) Obverse

**BATTLE OF MANILA BAY
MEDAL,**
Reverse

**WEST INDIES NAVAL
CAMPAIGN,**
Reverse of First Type

**WEST INDIES NAVAL
CAMPAIGN,**
(Sampson Medal)
Obverse

**WEST INDIES CAMPAIGN
MEDAL,**
Navy and Marine Corps

**SPANISH CAMPAIGN
MEDAL,**
Army

US Navy and Marine Corps who served aboard certain ships that took part in naval operations in the West Indies from April 27 to August 14, 1898.

The top suspension bar had the name of the recipient's ship, and forty-seven different engagement bars were authorized to be worn on the ribbon.

This medal is commonly called the "Sampson Medal" because a bust of the Admiral appears on the obverse, along with an inscription.

WEST INDIES CAMPAIGN MEDAL
(NAVY AND MARINE CORPS)

Authorized in 1908 to be awarded to members of the US Navy and Marine Corps who served aboard ships in the West Indies during the Spanish-American War.

This medal was rarely awarded because the recipients would have been entitled to the Naval Campaign Medal, (the "Sampson Medal") and the two awards could not be given for the same service. For this reason the medal was later discontinued.

SPANISH CAMPAIGN MEDAL
(ARMY)

Authorized in January 1905, and awarded for the following Army service during the War with Spain in 1898: Cuba, May 11 to July 17; Puerto Rico, July 24 to August 13; and the Philippine Islands, July 24 to August 13. The obverse has a castle with round corner towers, (taken from the arms of Spain) within the inscription. The medal ribbon was originally the color of the flag of Spain: red, yellow and blue. This was changed in 1913, in deference to a then friendly nation to the current ribbon of yellow and blue.

SPANISH CAMPAIGN MEDAL
(NAVY AND MARINE CORPS)

Authorized in 1908 for award to officers and men of the US Navy and Marine Corps for service afloat in the theater of active naval operations, or on shore in Cuba, Puerto Rico, the Philippines or Guam between May and August 16, 1898.

SPANISH WAR SERVICE MEDAL

Authorized on July 9, 1918 as an award for military personnel who served with the Army between April 20, 1898 and April 11, 1899, but were not eligible for the Spanish Campaign Medal. This medal is sometimes called the "National Guard Medal" because most of the recipients were members of these units. The obverse features a Roman sword on a tablet with the inscription, "For Service in the Spanish War", surrounded by a wreath.

AMERICAN OCCUPATION FORCES IN THE ISLANDS

After the peace treaty with Spain additional American forces were sent to Cuba, Puerto Rico, Guam and the Philippine Islands. The force sent Guam set up a military Naval Base, troops sent to Puerto Rico stayed on the Island for four months, while the force in Cuba remained until 1902. Those sent to the Philippines found themselves involved in another war, which is discussed in the next section.

ARMY OF CUBA OCCUPATION MEDAL

Established in 1915 for service with the Army of occupation in Cuba from July 18, 1898 to May 20, 1902, this Medal was designed by Heraldic Section of the US Army. On the obverse is the Cuban Republic coat of arms with wreath and fasces.

ARMY OF PUERTO RICO OCCUPATION MEDAL

Authorized in 1919 for service with the Army of occupation in Puerto Rico from August 14 to December 10, 1898, and designed by the Heraldic Section of the Army, using the original design of Francis D. Millet as used on the Spanish Campaign. The only change was the new legend at the top.

■ EXPEDITIONARY MEDALS ■ OF THE NAVY AND MARINE CORPS

The authorization for awarding these medals did not take place for a number of years, but since some of the operations covered by these awards occurred at the end of the 19th century, they are usually placed right after the Civil War medals for their respective branches.

MARINE CORPS EXPEDITIONARY MEDAL

Originally created as a ribbon bar only in 1919, the medal

**SPANISH CAMPAIGN
MEDAL,**
Navy and Marine Corps

**SPANISH WAR SERVICE
MEDAL**

**ARMY OF CUBA
OCCUPATION MEDAL**

was authorized on March 1, 1929. It is awarded to members of the Marine Corps who have engaged in operations against armed opposition on foreign territory, or who have served in circumstances which merit recognition but for which no campaign medal is awarded.

Designed by Walker Hancock, the obverse has a Marine with full pack charging with fixed bayonet, wave scrolls at the base, and the word "Expeditions", around the edge.

Additional expeditions are indicated by wearing a bronze star on the ribbon of this medal.

NAVY EXPEDITIONARY MEDAL

Authorized on August 15, 1936, and awarded to officers and enlisted men for service in expeditions and circumstances meriting special recognition for which no other medal is awarded.

The obverse shows a sailor beaching a boat containing an officer and Marines with a flag of the United States, and the word, "Expeditions".

NAVY AND MARINE CORPS EXPEDITIONS

The places and dates of expeditions for which the Marine Corps and Navy Expeditionary Medals are awarded illustrate the widely varying theaters of operation over the years. They include: Abyssinia, China, Colombia, Cuba, Dominican Republic, Egypt, Hawaiian Islands, Korea, Nicaragua, Panama, Philippine Islands, Russia, Samoa, Syria and Turkey.

Recently these medals were re-issued for certain expeditions that are not covered by the Armed Forces Expeditionary Medal. These include service in Cuba, Thailand, Indian Ocean/Iran and Lebanon. No person receives both Expeditionary medals for the same period of service.

■ THE PHILIPPINE ■ INSURRECTION, 1899–1913

The occupation troops that landed in the Philippines after the Spanish-American War found that the inhabitants wanted to have complete freedom, and looked upon the

**ARMY OF PORTO RICO
OCCUPATION MEDAL**

**MARINE CORPS
EXPEDITIONARY MEDAL**

**MARINE CORPS
EXPEDITIONARY MEDAL,**
with the rare "WAKE
Island" bar, and letter
"W" for service in defense
of the Island from
December 7 to December
22, 1941.

American troops as simply replacing the Spanish as their rulers. On February 4, 1899, Philippine patriots launched an assault against the American troops in Manila, and started a costly guerrilla war that lasted many years. On July 4, 1902 a civil government replaced the military one. Hostilities, however, continued in some places until 1913.

ARMY PHILIPPINE CAMPAIGN MEDAL

Authorized in 1905, and awarded to officers and enlisted men of the Army for service in the Philippine Islands during the insurrection. It was extended to cover actions in various parts of the islands through to 1913.

The obverse features a coconut palm tree, representing the character of the Philippines and a lamp and scales of Justice, symbolizing enlightenment under United States rule. The words, "Philippine Insurrection" and the date "1899" complete the design.

PHILIPPINE CAMPAIGN MEDAL
(NAVY AND MARINE CORPS)

Authorized by Congress in 1908 as an award for Navy

and Marine Corps officers and men who served aboard ships in Philippine waters, or performed duties ashore during various specified periods between February 1899 and November 1905, or for those who served ashore in Mindanao.

The obverse shows the Old gate in Manila City, and has the inscription "Philippine Campaign, 1899–1903." The original red and yellow ribbon was changed in 1913 to the current ribbon of blue and red, which is the same as the Army ribbon.

PHILIPPINE CONGRESSIONAL MEDAL

Authorized on June 29, 1906 and awarded to members of the Army who volunteered to remain beyond their discharge date to help suppress the insurrection, and who were ashore in the Philippines between February 4, 1899 and July 4, 1902. Using current standards, however, this medal would be considered an individual merit award.

The reverse of this medal has the words "For Patriotism, Fortitude, and Loyalty" within a wreath of laurel leaves and oak leaves, joined with a bow knot.

**NAVY EXPEDITIONARY
MEDAL**

**PHILIPPINE CAMPAIGN
MEDAL,**
Army

**PHILIPPINE CAMPAIGN
MEDAL,**
Navy and Marine Corps

■ THE BOXER REBELLION, ■
1900–1901 AND OTHER
CAMPAIGNS

Resentment against foreign interests exploded in China in 1900, when a revolt by a centuries-old secret society, *I Ho Ch'una*, the "Fists of Righteous Harmony", better known as the "Boxers", acted to rid China of all foreigners. They were eventually joined by Imperial troops, and laid siege to the International Legations in Peking. An International force known as the Peking Relief Expedition, composed of troops from Great Britain, France, Italy, Germany, Austria, Russia, Japan and the United States, relieved the settlements and crushed the rebellion by the following year, 1901.

CHINA CAMPAIGN MEDAL
(ARMY)

Authorized in 1905 and awarded for Army service ashore in China with the Expedition from June 20, 1900 to May 27, 1901.

The obverse has the Imperial Chinese dragon within the inscription, "China Relief Expedition 1900–1901."

CHINA RELIEF EXPEDITION MEDAL
(NAVY AND MARINE CORPS)

Authorized on June 27, 1908 and awarded to officers and enlisted men of the Navy and Marine Corps who served ashore in China between May 24, 1900 and May 27, 1901.

The obverse shows the *Chien Men*, the main gate of the walled city of Peking, with the Imperial dragon below, surrounded by the legend and date. The original ribbon was yellow with narrow black stripes near each edge, but this was changed to the current ribbon in 1913.

PACIFICATION OF CUBA, 1906–1909

American troops withdrew from Cuba when a Cuban Republic was formed in 1904. Political, economic and social difficulties soon led to insurrection, and the new government appealed to the United States for intervention. American troops were landed in Cuba in September

**PHILIPPINE
CONGRESSIONAL MEDAL**

CHINA CAMPAIGN MEDAL,
Army

CHINA RELIEF EXPEDITION,
Navy and Marine Corps

**CHINA RELIEF EXPEDITION
MEDAL**
with rare 1901 date.

**CUBAN PACIFICATION
MEDAL,**
Army

CUBAN PACIFICATION,
Navy and Marine Corps

NICARAGUAN CAMPAIGN MEDAL,
Navy and Marine Corps

MEXICAN SERVICE MEDAL,
Army

1906, a provisional government was formed and peace restored. The troops were withdrawn in 1909, after an election and the establishment of a new government.

CUBAN PACIFICATION MEDAL
(ARMY)

Authorized in 1909 for officers and men of the Army of Cuban Pacification who served in Cuba between October 6, 1906 and April 1, 1909. The Medal has on the obverse the Cuban coat of arms, with American soldiers standing at parade rest to either side of the shield. The words, "Cuban Pacification" appear above, and the dates below.

CUBAN PACIFICATION MEDAL
(NAVY AND MARINE CORPS)

Authorized on August 13, 1909 for officers and enlisted men who served ashore in Cuba or aboard designated ships from September 12, 1906, to April 1, 1907.

The obverse has a figure representing America, carrying a flag and offering an olive branch to a Cuban, with a dove overhead, surrounded by the legend.

In 1912 the Nicaraguan government requested United States aid in suppressing a revolution. An expedition force of eight ships carrying additional Marines was dispatched and landed in July 1912. After a series of small engagements, the revolutionary forces were defeated, and the troops were withdrawn on November 2, 1912.

NICARAGUAN CAMPAIGN MEDAL
(NAVY AND MARINE CORPS)

Authorized on September 22, 1913 for officers and enlisted men of the Navy and Marine Corps who served ashore or on the eight ships of the expedition from August 28 to November 2, 1912. The obverse shows the volcano, Mount Momotombo, rising from Lake Managua in a tropical setting, and the legend, "Nicaraguan Campaign" and date "1912".

■ TROUBLES AND ■ EXPEDITIONS TO MEXICO, 1911–1917

Turmoil following the Mexican Revolution of 1910 led to numerous battles and engagements between the United States and Mexican forces from 1911 to 1917, when the government was stabilized.

MEXICAN SERVICE MEDAL
(ARMY)

Authorized in 1917 for members of the Army and National Guard for service in expeditions or engagements in Mexico, or along the border in Texas and Arizona, during the period 1911 to 1917. The obverse has a yucca plant in bloom and mountains in the background.

MEXICAN SERVICE MEDAL
(NAVY AND MARINE CORPS)

Authorized on February 11, 1918 for officers and enlisted men of the Navy and Marine Corps who served on shore during the Vera Cruz Expedition, April 21–23, 1914. Also awarded to other officers and men of the Navy and Marine Corps who participated in engagements between United States and Mexican armed forces.

The obverse features the old castle of San Juan de Ulloa in Veracruz harbor, and around this the words, "Mexico" and dates "1911–1917", with branches of cactus between them.

■ SERVICE IN HAITI, ■ 1915–1916

After a long period of civil strife in Haiti, American Navy and Marine Corps forces were sent to Haiti at the request of France. Some order was restored and a treaty ratified in 1916 providing for Marines to stay in Haiti to train native troops. This occupation lasted until 1934.

HAITIAN CAMPAIGN MEDAL, 1915
(NAVY AND MARINE CORPS)

Authorized on June 22, 1917 for award to members of the Navy and Marine Corps who served in Haiti, or were attached to specified ships, between July 9 and December 5, 1915.

The obverse shows a view from the sea of mountains of Cape Haitien on the Island, and the inscription, "Haitian Campaign, 1915". There is also a medal with the date "1916" which should be considered as unofficial.

■ TROUBLE IN THE ■ DOMINICAN REPUBLIC IN 1916

The fighting between political factions in the Dominican Republic reached a climax in May of 1916, and United

MEXICAN SERVICE MEDAL,
Navy and Marine Corps

HAITIAN CAMPAIGN MEDAL,
Navy and Marine Corps

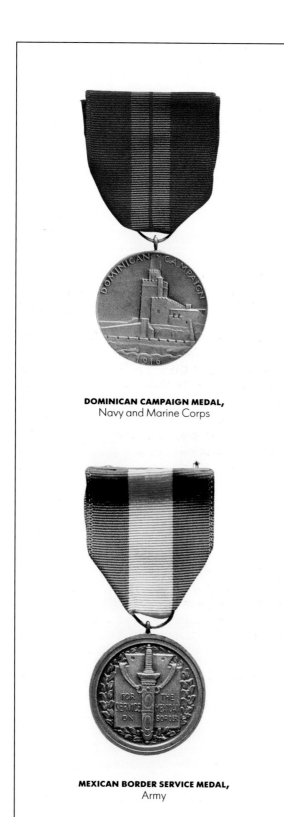

DOMINICAN CAMPAIGN MEDAL,
Navy and Marine Corps

MEXICAN BORDER SERVICE MEDAL,
Army

States Marines and Sailors were landed to protect American lives and property. They remained until December when order was restored.

DOMINICAN CAMPAIGN MEDAL, 1916
(NAVY AND MARINE CORPS)

Authorized on December 29, 1921, and awarded to officers of the Navy and Marine Corps who served in the Dominican Republic or attached to specific ships from May 5 to December 4, 1916.

Designed by A.A. Weinman, on the obverse is the "Tower of Homage" in the capital city, with sea wall and waves, and the inscription, "Dominican Campaign" and the date "1916"

■ SERVICE ON THE MEXICAN ■ BORDER, 1916–1917

From January 1, 1916 to April 6, 1917, a large portion of the regular Army and about 150,000 National Guardsmen took part in service and training on the Mexican Border. A medal was awarded for this service, usually to members of the National Guard because most Army troops had already received the Mexican Service Medal.

MEXICAN BORDER SERVICE MEDAL

Established on July 9, 1918 and awarded to members of the National Guard who served on the Mexican Border from May 9, 1916 and March 24, 1917. Also awarded to regular Army members who served with the Border Patrol from January 1, 1916 to April 6, 1917.

The same design used on the Spanish War Service Medal was used with a new inscription.

CHAPTER ELEVEN
CAMPAIGN MEDALS
1917–1989

■ AMERICA'S PART IN ■ WORLD WAR I

In 1914 most of Europe and many other parts of the world erupted in the global conflict of World War I. The United States remained neutral until April 6, 1917, when it declared war on Germany. The first American troops landed in France in June.

It had been the custom for nations to bestow medals on the personnel of their Allies, but since the size of the respective armies was now so immense, such an exchange of medals was impracticable. So it was decided that each of the victorious Allies would have a similar medal, which would feature a symbolic figure of Victory, and all would have the identical double rainbow ribbon. Since each country selected its own artist, these designs are quite different. It is a good way to start a collection to get Victory medals from each Allied nation.

▒▒▒▒ THE VICTORY MEDAL, WORLD WAR I ▒▒▒▒
(ALL SERVICES)

Authorized in 1919 for award to officers and enlisted men of the United States armed forces who had an honorable record for active duty between April 6, 1917 and November 11, 1918 or for service with the Allied Expeditionary Force (AEF) in European Russia, November 11, 1918 to August 5, 1919, and in Siberia, November 23, 1918 to April 1, 1920.

Designed by James E. Fraser, the obverse shows a female winged figure with shield and sword symbolic of Victory.

A unique feature of the Victory Medal was the adoption of clasps to be worn on the suspension ribbon of the medal. The Army adopted thirteen battle clasps to indicate participation in a major campaign, and a Defensive Sector clasp. They also created five service clasps with the name of countries — they were awarded to persons not entitled to battle clasps. These clasps are worn on the medal ribbon, and are represented by small bronze stars on the ribbon bars. The Navy also authorized suspension service clasps for Navy and Marine Corps personnel, though members of these units that served with the Army would receive the battle clasps for their combat service.

The Navy clasps were issued for service with a particular type of ship or unit, or for service in a particular area. This is indicated by what is on the bar. They are different from the Army clasps, being wider in design and with a rope border.

A small Maltese cross in bronze was authorized for Navy and Marine Corps personnel to indicate service with the AEF in France that did not include entitlement to a battle clasp.

Troops of the victorious Allies were stationed as Occupation troops in Germany and certain areas of Austria-Hungary after the Armistice was signed. American troops stayed in these occupied areas for a long period, not leaving until 1923, and appropriate Medals were awarded.

▒▒▒▒ ARMY OF OCCUPATION OF GERMANY ▒▒▒▒ MEDAL

Established on November 21, 1941 and awarded to all officers and enlisted men of the Army of Occupation who served in Germany or Austria-Hungary from November 12, 1918 to July 11, 1923. It was also awarded to members of the Navy and Marine Corps who served ashore during the same time and in the same areas. The medal features the profile of the commanding general of the Armies, General John J. Pershing, with the four stars of his rank above.

■ HAITI 1919–1921 ■ AND OTHER CAMPAIGNS

Troubles in Haiti in 1919 created the need for an Expeditionary force of Navy and Marine Corps personnel to help the Gendarmerie d'Haiti fight thousands of outlaws and restore order and stability to the Island.

HAITIAN CAMPAIGN MEDAL, 1919–1920

(NAVY AND MARINE CORPS)

Authorized on December 29, 1921 and awarded to officers and enlisted men of the Navy and Marine Corps who were engaged in operations in Haiti or attached to specified ships serving in Haitian waters between April 1, 1919 and June 15, 1920.

Designed by Bailey, Banks and Biddle, using the same design for the 1915 Haitian Campaign Medal with the date, "1915" replaced by "1919–1920".

Over the next twenty years, Marines and Navy personnel were actively engaged in a number of expeditions around the world, including a return to Nicaragua in 1926 for service that was to last until 1933.

HAITIAN CAMPAIGN MEDAL
as awarded to members of the Navy and Marine Corps who served in Haiti in the 1915 campaign and were awarded the earlier medal, and who also served in the 1919–1920 campaign, for which they were awarded the bar as shown. Recipients of the medal with bar wore a bronze star on the ribbon bar.

SECOND NICARAGUAN CAMPAIGN MEDAL

(NAVY AND MARINE CORPS)

Authorized on November 8, 1929 and awarded to officers and enlisted men of the Navy and Marine Corps who served on shore in Nicaragua or aboard ships in Nicaraguan waters between August 27, 1926 and January 2, 1933. It was also awarded to members of the Army who cooperated in the operations.

Troubles and unrest in China from 1927 to 1939 led to a build-up of American forces in that country which led to the creation of the next two medals for services in China.

YANGTZE SERVICE MEDAL

(NAVY AND MARINE CORPS)

Authorized on April 28, 1930, the Medal was awarded to members of the Navy and Marine Corps who served on shore at Shanghai or in the valley of the Yangtze with landing forces between September 3, 1926 and October 21, 1927 and again from March 1, 1930 to December 31, 1932, or who served on ships during these periods.

CHINA SERVICE MEDAL

(NAVY AND MARINE CORPS)

Authorized on August 23, 1940 , and awarded to officers and men of the Navy and Marine Corps who participated in operations ashore in China, or were attached to certain ships in support of these operations between July 7, 1937 and September 7, 1939. The obverse shows a Chinese junk under full sail, with the inscription, "China Service" around the edge.

It should also be noted that the Marine Corps Expeditionary Medal and the Navy Expeditionary Medals were issued for some service in China in the same time periods.

A limited Emergency was proclaimed by the President of the United States with the outbreak of World War II on September 8, 1939. Proclaiming this Emergency allowed the President to greatly increase the size of the Armed Forces, and to step up the building of ships, planes and aircraft. The proclamation also established the draft, allowing the government to put civilians in uniform. The following Medal was authorized for service during this pre-War period.

AMERICAN DEFENSE SERVICE MEDAL

Authorized on June 28, 1941 and awarded to members of the armed forces "for service during the limited emer-

**VICTORY MEDAL WORLD
WAR ONE,**
(with Navy Service Bar)

THE VICTORY MEDAL,
World War One, (with
Army Bars)

**ARMY OF OCCUPATION
MEDAL**

**HAITIAN CAMPAIGN
MEDAL,**
1919–1920 Navy and
Marines

**SECOND NICARAGUAN
CAMPAIGN MEDAL,**
Navy and Marines

YANGTZE SERVICE MEDAL,
Navy and Marine Corps

CHINA SERVICE MEDAL,
Navy and Marine Corps

**AMERICAN DEFENSE
SERVICE MEDAL**

**AMERICAN DEFENSE
SERVICE MEDAL**
with Navy "Patrol" bar

gency proclaimed by the President on September 8, 1939, or during the unlimited emergency proclaimed by the President on May 27, 1941." These words appear on the reverse side of the Medal.

On the obverse, a female figure representing Liberty is shown in a attitude of defense, holding shield and sword, standing on live oak, with the inscription above. Several clasps were awarded with this medal.

■ THE UNITED STATES IN ■ WORLD WAR TWO

On December 7, 1942, when the Japanese attacked Pearl Harbor, the United States became part of the Allied effort in the War that had been going on since 1939. World War II was a global conflict on a scale which mankind had never before even imagined. Forty million lives were lost before the final capitulation of the Axis powers on September 2, 1945.

Armed forces of the United States served all over the world, and it was decided that medals would be awarded for service in one of three carefully bounded and defined areas. The three areas taken together encompass the entire globe.

Three different campaign medals and a World War II Victory Medal were issued for service in the armed forces of the United States during World War II.

A bronze campaign star was authorized to be worn on the ribbon bar of the medal for service in a specified campaign or operation within a campaign. A silver star is worn in lieu of five bronze stars. A bronze arrowhead was authorized by the Army to be worn on the campaign medals to denote invasion participation. The Navy authorized the wearing of a small Marine Corps device, to indicate Naval personnel serving with Marine Corps units.

AMERICAN CAMPAIGN MEDAL

Authorized on November 6, 1942, and awarded to all members of the armed forces who, between December 7, 1941 and March 2, 1946, served on land or aboard certain ships for one year within the continental limits of the United States or thirty days service outside the continental limits of the United States but within the American theater of operations.

AMERICAN CAMPAIGN
MEDAL

EUROPEAN-AFRICAN-
MIDDLE EASTERN
CAMPAIGN MEDAL

ASIATIC-PACIFIC
CAMPAIGN MEDAL

Designed by the Army Heraldic Section, the obverse shows a Navy cruiser, a B-24 bomber and a submarine and waves. In the background are buildings representing the arsenal of democracy, above this the inscription "American Campaign."

EUROPEAN-AFRICAN-MIDDLE EASTERN CAMPAIGN MEDAL

Authorized on November 6, 1942, and awarded to all members of the armed forces of the United States who served in the prescribed area or aboard certain ships for a thirty day period between December 7, 1941, and November 8, 1945. The obverse shows a landing with LST, (Landing Ship Tanks) smaller craft and troops with an airplane overhead, above this the inscription, "European-African-Middle Eastern Campaign."

ASIATIC-PACIFIC CAMPAIGN MEDAL

Authorized on November 6, 1942, and awarded to all members of the armed forces of the United States for thirty days active service in the prescribed area or aboard certain ships between December 7, 1941 and November 8, 1945. The obverse shows troops landing in a tropical scene, with palm trees, and with ships in the background and planes overhead, above this is the inscription, "Asiatic-Pacific Campaign."

Unfortunately, the custom of awarding bars indicating the campaign or service as used on the Victory Medal of World War I was not continued. When one finds the Asiatic-Pacific Campaign medal with three stars, little else is known.

WORLD WAR TWO VICTORY MEDAL

Authorized on July 6, 1945 and awarded to all members of the United States armed forces who served on active duty at any time between December 7, 1941 and December 31, 1946. This medal was also awarded to members of the Philippine armed forces.

Designed by the Army Heraldic Section, the obverse shows a female figure representing Liberation, her foot resting on a helmet, she holds a broken sword. Rays behind the figure and the inscription, "World War II" complete the design.

**WOMEN'S ARMY CORPS
SERVICE MEDAL**

**ARMY OCCUPATION
SERVICE MEDAL**

**WORLD WAR TWO VICTORY
MEDAL**

KOREAN SERVICE MEDAL

**NAVY OCCUPATION
SERVICE MEDAL**

**MEDAL FOR HUMANE
ACTION**
(Berlin Airlift)

■ WOMEN'S ARMY CORPS ■
SERVICE MEDAL

Authorized in 1943 and awarded for service in the Women's Army Auxiliary Corps between July 20, 1942 and August 31, 1943, and for service in the Women's Army corps from September 1, 1943 to September 2, 1945.

The obverse shows the head of Athena, goddess of victory and wisdom, on a sheathed sword, crossed with oak leaves and a palm branch, and the inscription, "Women's Army Corps".

■ OCCUPATION SERVICE ■
1945–1955

At the close of hostilities it was necessary to station troops in the occupied territories for a number of years, and both the Army and Navy issued medals for personnel serving in the occupied zones. Service in Europe dates from May 9, 1945, and in Asia from September 3, 1945. The occupied territories were: Austria, Germany, Italy, Berlin and Japan.

■ ARMY OF OCCUPATION MEDAL ■

Authorized in 1946, this is awarded for thirty days consecutive service in any of the occupied territories after World War II. Clasps inscribed with the words, "Germany" and "Japan" were authorized to be worn with the medal. The Berlin Airlift Device was also authorized for personnel for 90 consecutive days service with a unit credited with participation in the Berlin Airlift between June 26, 1948 and September 30, 1949.

The obverse shows the Remagen bridge abutments, symbolic of Europe, above this are the words, "Army Of Occupation". The reverse shows Mount Fujiyama, symbolic of Asia.

■ NAVY OCCUPATION MEDAL ■

Authorized on January 22, 1947 for award to members of the Navy, Marine Corps and Coast Guard for thirty consecutive days service in occupation zones after World War II.

On the obverse is a representation of Neptune riding an animal with the head of a horse and the tail of a serpent, holding a trident in the right hand and pointing with the left, below are waves and the words, "Occupation Service".

■ MEDAL FOR HUMANE ACTION ■

Authorized on July 20, 1949 the Medal was awarded to members of the Armed Forces of the United States assigned to the Berlin Airlift for 120 or more days during the period June 26, 1948 and September 30, 1949. This medal was also awarded to foreign armed forces and to U.S. and foreign civilians who were recommended for meritorious participation in the Berlin Airlift.

The obverse features a C-54 airplane within a wreath of wheat and in the center the coat of arms of the city of Berlin.

■ POST-WAR SERVICE ■
MEDALS

The Berlin Airlift Medal for Humane Action was the first of many medals that would indicate service in the so-called "Cold War" between the super powers. Some of these "Cold War" conflicts — Korea and Vietnam, for example — were long and bitter conflicts, causing hundreds of thousands of casualties, but they have, arguably, avoided a global conflict between East and West.

■ THE KOREAN WAR ■
1950–1953

The war in Korea began with the North Korean Invasion of South Korea on June 27, 1950. The United States decided to send troops to aid the South Koreans, and on July 7th the United Nations adopted a resolution that would make this conflict a test of the powers of the U.N. to halt and repel aggression against any member states. China entered the War in November to save the North Koreans, who had been beaten and lost most of their territory.

In September 1951, the Korean War had reached a stalemate and became a war of the trenches and outposts, similar to World War I. The situation continued for two more desperate, bloody and costly years until a truce was signed on June 27, 1953.

■ KOREAN SERVICE MEDAL ■

Authorized on November 8, 1950 and awarded to members of the United States armed forces for thirty consecutive days of service in Korea between June 27, 1950 and July 27, 1954. Also awarded certain ships in Korean waters, units engaged in aerial missions over Korea, and

NATIONAL DEFENSE SERVICE MEDAL

ARMED FORCES EXPEDITIONARY MEDAL

units in direct support of the effort.

The obverse has a Korean gateway encircled by the inscription, "Korean Service". A series of campaign stars were authorized for award with this medal.

NATIONAL DEFENSE SERVICE MEDAL

Authorized on April 22, 1953 and amended on January 11, 1966, this Medal was awarded for honorable active military service as a member of the United States Armed Forces, including the Coast Guard, between June 27, 1950 and July 27, 1954, (Korean War Period) and between January 1, 1961 and August 14, 1974, (Vietnam War Period). The obverse has an American bald eagle with inverted wings standing on a sword and palm branch with the inscription, "National Defense" above.

A series of US Military operations and expeditions that covered a period from 1958 to 1983 and took place all over the world led to the creation of a new medal called the Armed Forces Expeditionary Medal. Operations in theaters such as Lebanon in 1958, to Grenada in 1983, were included in the long list of expeditions.

ARMED FORCES EXPEDITIONARY MEDAL

Authorized on December 4, 1961, and awarded to members of the United States Armed Forces who after July 1, 1958 participated in US military operations, US operations in direct support of the United Nations, or US operations of assistance for friendly foreign nations or in danger from hostile actions.

The obverse has an eagle with wings raised perched on a compass rose, with rays between the arms, surrounded by the inscription, "Armed Forces Expeditionary Service".

■ THE VIETNAM WAR, ■ 1962–1973

The official policy of the United States regarding Vietnam was that the government of South Vietnam should remain free and non-communist — very much like its position towards South Korea in 1950. Military and Political advisors had been serving in South Vietnam since 1958 and a gradual build-up of these forces took place. By 1962 the United States were committed to a War that would last until 1973, a War that would cost over fifty thousand American lives.

∎ VIETNAM SERVICE MEDAL

Authorized on July 89, 1965 and awarded to all service members of the Armed Forces of the United States who, between July 4, 1965 and March 28, 1973, served in Vietnam and the contiguous waters and airspace, in Thailand, Laos or Cambodia or airspace in direct support of military operations in Vietnam. Personnel previously awarded the Armed Forces Expeditionary Medal for services between July 1958 and July, 1963 could exchange these medals for the Vietnam Service Medal.

Designed by Thomas H. Jones, on the obverse is the figure of a dragon behind a grove of bamboo trees, below this the words, "Republic of Vietnam Service".

∎ CIVILIAN SERVICE IN VIETNAM MEDAL

Authorized on December 18, 1967 by the Department of State to recognize the service of civilian employees of the government serving in Vietnam for one year, or for a lesser period if this service had been discontinued due to injury or disability from hostile action.

The obverse shows a striking representation of an Oriental dragon entwined around a flaming torch of knowledge, with the words, "Vietnam Service."

∎ HUMANITARIAN SERVICE MEDAL

Authorized on January 19, 1977, this is awarded to members of the Armed Forces of the United States who, after April 1, 1975, distinguished themselves by meritorious direct participation in a significant military act or operation of humanitarian nature, or who have rendered a service to mankind.

The obverse of the medal has within a circle a right hand pointing diagonally upward with open palm, (symbolizing a giving or helping hand). Operations which merit consideration for the Medal include disaster, flood, tornado and earthquake relief work, or rescue operations anywhere in the world.

∎ THE DOMINICAN ∎ REPUBLIC INTERVENTION, APRIL, 1965

President Lyndon Johnson committed elements of the 82nd Airborne Division and Marine Corps units to the Dominican Republic in April 1965 to stop the fighting and disturbances in that country, and to protect American citizens and property threatened by dissident groups.

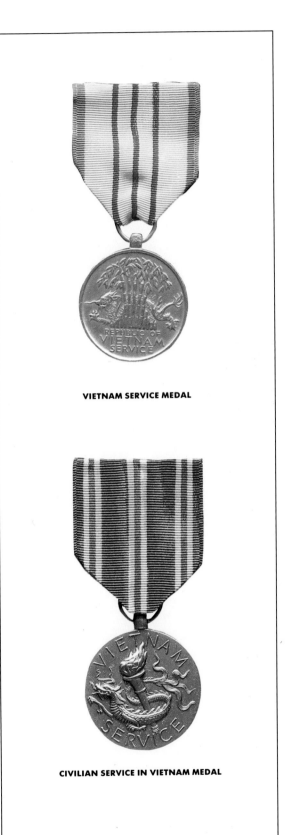

VIETNAM SERVICE MEDAL

CIVILIAN SERVICE IN VIETNAM MEDAL

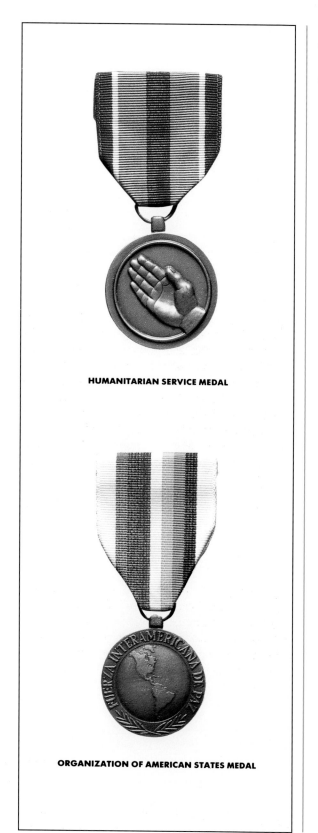

HUMANITARIAN SERVICE MEDAL

ORGANIZATION OF AMERICAN STATES MEDAL

President Johnson suggested that other countries of the OAS, (Organization of American States) assume some responsibilities, and it was proposed that a medal be struck to recognize their participation.

THE ORGANIZATION OF AMERICAN STATES MEDAL

Designed by the Institute of Heraldry in anticipation of its award to foreign nationals as well as United States troops involved in the Intervention in the Dominican Republic, April 28, 1965 to September 21, 1966. On the obverse in the center is a map of North and South America within a disk, round this the words, "Fuerza InterAmericana De Paz", (InterAmerican Force For Peace) and at the bottom crossed olive branches. On the reverse the words, "Al Merito" (For Merit) appear.

However on submission, the Department of the Army recommended disapproval of the medal. Nevertheless, copies of this "medal that never was" do exist in some collections.

CHAPTER TWELVE
RIBBON BARS

Like the Unit Citations previously mentioned, most of the following awards are ribbon bars only. There has never been a medal designed for these awards, and they are usually issued for service in a particular area (overseas or difficult duty) or to indicate some military specialty, attendance and/or graduation from a selected military program.

OVERSEAS SERVICE RIBBON
(ARMY)

Authorized by the Secretary of the Army on April 10, 1981, and awarded, effective August 1, 1981, to all members of the Regular Army, Army National Guard, and Army Reserve for successful completion of an overseas tour. The Overseas Service Ribbon is not awarded for service that is recognized by another service medal or ribbon. Numerical devices will be awarded and worn on the ribbon to denote subsequent overseas tours of duty.

RESERVE COMPONENT OVERSEAS TRAINING RIBBON

Authorized by the Secretary of the Army on July 11, 1984, the ribbon is awarded to members of the US Army Reserve Components for successful completion of Annual Training or Active Duty for Training for a period of not less than ten consecutive duty days on foreign soil.

The ribbon has a very unusual vertical stripe pattern that is almost identical to the Merchant Marine Combat Bar.

SEA SERVICE DEPLOYMENT RIBBON

This award was approved by the Secretary of the Navy on May 22, 1980. It recognizes the unique and demanding nature of sea service and the arduous duty attendant with such service deployments. The award of the ribbon was made retrospective to 15 August 1974. It is presented to officers and enlisted personnel of the US Navy and Marine Corps assigned to US (including Hawaii and Alaska) home-ported ships and overseas ships deploying units or Fleet Marine Force (FMF) commands, for 12 months' accumulated sea duty or duty with FMF which includes at least one 90-consecutive-day deployment.

NAVY AND MARINE CORPS OVERSEAS SERVICE RIBBON

Authorized by the Secretary of the Navy on June 3, 1987, and awarded to officers and enlisted personnel of the US Navy and Marine Corps on active duty for 12 consecutive months or accumulated duty at an overseas duty station and to officers and enlisted personnel of the US Naval Reserve and Marine Corps Reserve for 30 consecutive days or 45 cumulative days of Active Duty for training or Temporary Active Duty.

NAVY FLEET MARINE FORCE RIBBON

Authorized by the Secretary of the Navy on September 1, 1984. The Navy Fleet Marine Force Ribbon was established to recognize officers and enlisted men of the US Navy who serve with the Marine Corps and demonstrate exceptional Navy qualification in providing support in a combat environment. Officers and enlisted personnel must serve a minimum of 12 months' duty with the FMF, satisfactorily complete Marine Corps Essential Subjects Test and satisfactorily pass the USMC Physical Fitness Test.

AIR FORCE OVERSEAS RIBBON
(LONG TOUR)

Authorized by the US Air Force on October 12, 1980, this ribbon is awarded to US Air Force and Air Force Reserve service members credited with completion of an overseas long tour on or after September 1, 1980. It is not awarded for service that is recognized by another service medal.

AIR FORCE OVERSEAS RIBBON
(SHORT TOUR)

Authorized by the Chief of Staff, US Air Force on October 12, 1980. This ribbon is awarded to US Air Force and Air Force Reserve service members who are credited with completion of an overseas short tour after September 1, 1980.

COAST GUARD SEA SERVICE RIBBON

Established on March 3, 1984, by the Commandant, US Coast Guard, this is awarded to Coast Guard Personnel who have completed a total of two years' sea duty on a Coast Guard cutter 65 feet or more in length in an active status, in commission or in service.

NCO PROFESSIONAL DEVELOPMENT RIBBON
(ARMY)

Authorized on April 10, 1981, this ribbon is awarded, effective August 1, 1981, to all enlisted service members of the Regular US Army, Army National Guard, and Army Reserve for successful completion of designated NCO professional development courses.

NAVY ARCTIC SERVICE RIBBON

Established by the Chief of Naval Operations on June 3, 1987 and awarded to officers and enlisted personnel of the United States Naval Services and civilians of the United States who participate in operations in support of the Arctic Warfare Program. The time requirements are 28 days 8 consecutive or non-consecutive — adjacent to, on, under or over the Arctic ice from the marginal ice zone (MIZ) north.

ARMY SUPERIOR UNIT AWARD

Authorized by the Secretary of the Army on April 8, 1985, it is awarded by the Chief of Staff, US Army for outstanding meritorious performance of a unit of a uniquely difficult and challenging mission under extraordinary circumstances that involved the national interest during peacetime.

NAVAL RESERVE SEA SERVICE RIBBON

Authorized on 3 June 1987. It is awarded to officers and enlisted personnel of the United States Navy and Naval Reserve for active duty, selected reserve service or combination of service after 15 August 1974, aboard a Naval Reserve ship or its Reserve unit or an embarked active or reserve staff, for a cumulative total of 36 months.

ARMY SERVICE RIBBON

Authorized by the Secretary of the Army on April 10, 1981, this ribbon is awarded, effective August 1, 1981 to all service members of the Regular US Army, Army National Guard, and Army Reserve to indicate the successful completion of initial entry training.

AIR FORCE NCO ACADEMY GRADUATE RIBBON

Authorized on August 28, 1962, this ribbon is awarded to graduates of a certified US Air Force NCO (Non Commissioned Officer), PME, (Professional Military Education) school, phase III, IV and V. Award of the ribbon is retrospective for graduates of a certified NCO leadership school.

AIR FORCE BASIC MILITARY TRAINING HONOR GRADUATE RIBBON

Authorized by the Chief of Staff, US Air Force on April 3, 1976, this ribbon is awarded to honor graduates of BMT (Basic Military Training) who, after July 29, 1976, have demonstrated excellence in all phases of academic and military training and limited to the top 10 percent of the training flight.

AIR FORCE TRAINING RIBBON

Authorized by the Chief of Staff, US Air Force on October 12, 1980, this is awarded to members of the Air Force for the completion of initial accession training after August 14, 1974.

AIR FORCE SMALL ARMS EXPERT MARKSMAN RIBBON

Authorized on August 28, 1962, and awarded to all US Air Force service members who, after January 1, 1963, qualify as "expert" in small-arms marksmanship with either the M-16 rifle or .38, 9mm-caliber pistol.

COAST GUARD BASIC TRAINING HONOR GRADUATE RIBBON

Established on March 3, 1984, by the Commandant of the US Coast Guard, it is awarded, effective April 1, 1984, to members of the Coast Guard in the top three percent of each US Coast Guard recruit training graduating class.

COAST GUARD RESTRICTED DUTY RIBBON

Established on March 3, 1984 by the Commandant of the US Coast Guard. It is awarded to US Coast Guard service members who have completed a permanent change of station (PCS) tour of duty at a shore unit where accompanying dependents are not authorized.

COMMANDANT'S LETTER OF COMMENDATION RIBBON
(US COAST GUARD)

Among the oldest of the awards presented to members of the US Coast Guard, the Commandant's Letter of Commendation has always been in the form of letter or commendation certificate.

The ribbon bar was established on March 17, 1979 by the Commandant, to accompany the Letter of Commendation from the Commandant of the US Coast Guard. It is awarded members of the US Armed Forces, serving in any capacity with the US Coast Guard, for an act or service resulting in unusual or outstanding achievement.

COAST GUARD SPECIAL OPERATIONS SERVICE RIBBON

Authorized by the Commandant of the Coast Guard on July 1, 1987, this is awarded to members of the US Armed Forces, serving in any capacity with the Coast Guard and certain other individuals who participate in a special

U.S. NAVY EXPERT RIFLEMAN BADGE

U.S. NAVY EXPERT PISTOL SHOT BADGE

COAST GUARD EXPERT RIFLEMAN'S MEDAL

COAST GUARD EXPERT PISTOL SHOT MEDAL

operation of the Coast Guard, not involving combat after July 1, 1987, and when that operation is not recognized by another award.

■ AWARDS FOR ■ MARKSMANSHIP

▨▨▨ US NAVY EXPERT RIFLEMAN BADGE ▨▨▨

Established in 1920 to replace the Navy Sharpshooters Medal created in 1910. The medal was designed and struck at the US Mint.

Awarded to members of the United States Navy and Navy Reserve who qualify as Expert with either rifle or carbine firing a prescribed military rifle course, and issued by the Chief of Naval Personnel.

▨▨▨ US NAVY EXPERT PISTOL SHOT BADGE ▨▨▨

This award was created at the same time as the previous badge and is awarded to all personnel of the United States Navy and Navy Reserves who have qualified as expert pistol shots on prescribed courses.

▨▨▨ NAVY RIFLE AND PISTOL ▨▨▨ MARKSMANSHIP RIBBONS

Both the "Navy Pistol Marksmanship Ribbon" and the "Navy Rifle Marksmanship Ribbon" were established by the Secretary of the Navy on October 14, 1969 to provide for the Navy's increasing emphasis on small arms training and skill. The ribbons are an incentive for recognition of outstanding marksmanship performance.

▨▨▨ NAVY PISTOL MARKSMANSHIP ▨▨▨ RIBBON

The ribbon is dark blue with two thin light green stripes, one towards each edge. An unadorned ribbon signifies Marksman. The same ribbon with a bronze letter "S" is worn on the ribbon bar for sharpshooter qualification. Navy personnel who attain a first and second expert qualification wear the ribbon bar with a bronze "E". Upon attaining the third and final expert qualification, a silver "E" is attached to the ribbon.

▨▨▨ NAVY RIFLE MARKSMANSHIP RIBBON ▨▨▨

The ribbon bar is dark blue with three thin stripes of light green, one centered and one toward either edge. Qualification letters are worn on the ribbon, as with the above marksmanship ribbon.

▨▨▨ COAST GUARD EXPERT ▨▨▨ RIFLEMAN'S MEDAL

This medal, and the Expert Pistol badge following are qualification badges like the previous awards, but have always been referred to as medals in official correspondence. Awarded to personnel of the Coast Guard and the Coast Guard Reserves who have qualified as Expert with the military service rifle or carbine.

▨▨▨ COAST GUARD EXPERT ▨▨▨ PISTOL SHOT MEDAL

This medal is a qualification badge, authorized and created at the time as the Expert Rifleman's Medal. It is awarded to all personnel of the Coast Guard and Coast Guard Reserves who have qualified as Expert with the required military pistol.

▨▨▨ RESERVE COMPONENT OVERSEAS ▨▨▨ TRAINING RIBBON

Authorized by the Secretary of the Army in March 1989, this ribbon is authorized to members of US Army Reserve Component Units who have received specialized training in an overseas station, and whose service is not recognized by any other service medal or ribbon.

CHAPTER THIRTEEN

MEDALS FOR THE POLAR EXPLORATIONS

The following medals were created to commemorate US explorations of the polar regions and to honor the men who faced hazardous conditions and endured so much for the exploration of the unknown and the advancement of science.

THE ARCTIC EXPLORATION MEDAL, 1879–1882

Authorized by Congress on September 30, 1890, and awarded to survivors and next of kin of the ill-fated Arctic Expedition, 1879–1882. It was the first of a series of medals issued by the United States for Polar Expeditions. The top bar of the medal ribbon has the name of the ship, "JEANNETTE", and the medal is referred to as the "Jeannette Medal".

PEARY POLAR EXPEDITION MEDAL, 1908–1909

Authorized by Congress on January 28, 1944, and awarded to members of Admiral Robert E. Peary's Polar Expedition of 1908–1909. On April 6, 1909 Peary and four members of his crew claimed to be the first to reach the North Pole, and this is indicated by the inscription.

BYRD ANTARCTIC EXPEDITION MEDAL, 1928–1930

Authorized by Congress on May 23, 1930, the Medal was awarded to officers and men of the Byrd Antarctic Expedition of 1928–1930, when Byrd set up a base of operations called Little America, from which he made the first flight over the South Pole on November 29th. This medal was struck in Gold for Admiral Byrd and was also awarded in Gold, Silver and Bronze to other selected personnel involved with the Expedition.

SECOND BYRD ANTARCTIC EXPEDITION, 1933–1935

Authorized by Congress on June 6, 1936, and awarded to all personnel of the Second Byrd Expedition who spent the winter night (lasting six months) at the Little America base in Antarctica or who commanded either of the expedition ships used for transport and re-supply.

UNITED STATES ANTARCTIC EXPEDITION, 1939–1941

Authorized by Congress on September 24, 1945, this was awarded to officers and men of the First United States Antarctic Expedition of 1939–1941. Though under the command of Admiral Byrd it was not named after as it was an official government operation.

ANTARCTICA SERVICE MEDAL

Authorized by Congress on July 7, 1960, for award to members of the Armed Forces of the United States, citizens or resident aliens of the United States, who after January 1, 1946, served on the Antarctic continent or in support of US operations there.

WINTERED OVER

(BAR AND RIBBON DISK)

Established at the same time as the above medal, a clasp and disk were created to indicate that the recipient remained on the Antarctic continent during the winter months. The clasp worn on the medal ribbon is a framed rectangular bar bearing the words, "Wintered Over", and the disk, worn on the ribbon bar, has a representation of the Antarctic continent on it.

BYRD ANTARCTIC EXPEDITION MEDAL,
(1928–1930), Gold Medal (this medal was also
awarded in silver and bronze)

PEARY POLAR EXPEDITION MEDAL,
(1908–1909)

SECOND BYRD ANTARCTIC EXPEDITION,
(1933–1935)

**UNITED STATES ANTARCTIC EXPEDITION MEDAL IN
BRONZE**

UNITED STATES ANTARCTIC EXPEDITION,
(1939–41) in Gold (this medal was also awarded
in silver and bronze)

ANTARCTIC SERVICE MEDAL

**COAST GUARD ARCTIC
SERVICE MEDAL**

**NASA ORIGINAL
DISTINGUISHED SERVICE
MEDAL** (Obsolete)

**NASA ORIGINAL
EXCEPTIONAL SERVICE
MEDAL** (Obsolete)

COAST GUARD ARCTIC SERVICE MEDAL

Authorized by the Coast Guard on May 20, 1976, this is awarded to members of the US Coast Guard who have served aboard US Coast Guard ships or aircraft for a specified period within the Polar regions of the Arctic Circle, or who have participated in US Arctic Programs as determined by the Commandant.

The following medals are currently awarded for services in the Arctic and Antarctic regions. Though these operations are no longer considered expeditions, the same hazardous and difficult conditions exist for service in these areas.

NAVY ARCTIC SERVICE RIBBON

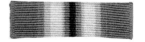

Established on June 3, 1987 by the Chief of Naval Operations, and awarded to officers and men of the US Naval Services and US Civilians who participate in operations in support of the Arctic Warfare Program.

■ THE NATIONAL ■ AERONAUTICS AND SPACE ADMINISTRATION

It was decided almost from the very beginning of NASA, that a decorations and awards system should be created to reward and recognize members and employees of the agency. These awards would be in the fields of personal heroism or endurance, notable scientific achievements and breakthroughs. Most of these decorations and awards were established by NASA on July 29, 1959.

NASA DISTINGUISHED SERVICE MEDAL
(FIRST DESIGN, NOW OBSOLETE)

Awarded for outstanding heroism and achievement in space, it is a circular gold medal and on the obverse is the official seal of NASA. In front is a wing-type vector representing an upward trajectory and direction and there is a orbit ring going around the planet. This is within a circle bearing the inscription, "National Aeronautics and Space Administration U.S.A.".

NASA DISTINGUISHED
SERVICE MEDAL

NASA EXCEPTIONAL
BRAVERY MEDAL

NASA OUTSTANDING
LEADERSHIP MEDAL

NASA EXCEPTIONAL SERVICE MEDAL
(FIRST DESIGN, NOW OBSOLETE)

This decoration was established and created at the same time as the DSM mentioned above. The Medal, in silver, is awarded for exceptional service to the agency.
NASA currently awards ten distinctive decorations, each one of which consists of a medal and ribbon, lapel emblem and a framed certificate bearing the official seal of NASA and signed by the Administrator.

THE CONGRESSIONAL SPACE MEDAL OF HONOR

This Medal was established by an Act of Congress on September 29, 1969 which authorized that the President may award, and present in the name of Congress, the Congressional Space Medal of Honor to any astronaut, civilian or military, who has distinguished himself or herself by exceptionally meritorious efforts and contributions to the welfare of the nation and of mankind.

NASA DISTINGUISHED SERVICE MEDAL

This decoration, created by NASA on July 29, 1959, is the highest award presented by the agency. It is awarded to any person in the Federal service who, by distinguished service, ability, or courage, has personally made a contribution representing substantial progress to aeronautical science or space exploration in the interests of the United States.

NASA EXCEPTIONAL BRAVERY MEDAL

Awarded for exemplary and courageous handling of an emergency in NASA program activities by an individual who, independent of personal danger, has acted to safeguard human life or government property; or for exemplary and courageous service by an individual in his performance, irrespective of personal danger, of an official task of importance to the mission of NASA.

NASA OUTSTANDING LEADERSHIP MEDAL

Awarded for notably outstanding leadership which has had a pronounced effect upon the aerospace, technological or administrative programs of NASA.

NASA EXCEPTIONAL SCIENTIFIC ACHIEVEMENT MEDAL

Awarded for unusually significant scientific contributions toward achievement of the aeronautical or space exploration goals of NASA, the Department of Defense or other government agencies.

NASA DISTINGUISHED PUBLIC SERVICE MEDAL

Awarded to individuals whose meritorious contributions produced results which measurably improved, expedited, or clarified administrative procedures, scientific progress, work methods, and other efforts related to the accomplishment of the mission of NASA. It is an award for those not employed by Federal government.

NASA PUBLIC SERVICE MEDAL

Awarded to any individual who is not an employee of the Federal Government or was not an employee during the period in which the service was performed, for exceptional contributions to the engineering design and development or management coordination of programs related to the accomplishment of the mission of NASA.

NASA EQUAL EMPLOYMENT OPPORTUNITY MEDAL

Awarded for outstanding achievement and material contribution to the goals of the Equal Employment Opportunity programs either within Government or within community organizations or groups relating to the mission of NASA.

NASA EXCEPTIONAL SERVICE MEDAL

Awarded for significant achievement or service characterized by unusual initiative or creative ability that clearly demonstrates substantial or unusual improvement in engineering, aeronautics, space flight and/or space related endeavors which contribute to the programs of NASA.

NASA EXCEPTIONAL ENGINEERING ACHIEVEMENT MEDAL

Awarded to members of NASA for unusually significant engineering contributions toward achievement of aeronautical or space exploration goals.

NASA SPACE FLIGHT MEDAL

This medal was created by the act of July 29, 1959, that created almost all of the awards of NASA. It is awarded to the crew members of the space shuttle program who have actually flown into outer space in one of these shuttle missions.

■ MEDALS OF THE UNITED ■ STATES MERCHANT MARINE

Ships of the United States Merchant Marine were serving in many dangerous areas and war zones from the outbreak of World War II on September 8, 1939, long before Pearl Harbor and America's entry into the conflict. They were strafed, bombed and torpedoed as they moved strategic supplies to Allied countries.

Even though the Merchant Marine was part of a civilian agency employing men who were not eligible for military awards, the hazardous and honorable service of the officers and ranks of the merchant fleets required recognition. The Maritime Commission developed their own system of awards, and if members left the merchant service to join the military, they were authorized to wear the ribbons of the Merchant Marine on their uniforms in honor of their service to the country.

So few medals were awarded by the Merchant Marine that they are considered rare. All are wonderful works of art, designed by one of America's finest sculptors, Paul Manship, who also designed the Navy Distinguished Service Medal.

MERCHANT MARINE DISTINGUISHED SERVICE MEDAL

Congress authorized the Maritime Commission to create and award this decoration on April 11, 1943. Awarded to any person in the US Merchant Marine, who, on or after September 3, 1939, distinguished himself by outstanding service in the line of duty, it is the highest decoration for heroism awarded by the Merchant Marine.

MERITORIOUS SERVICE MEDAL

Authorized on August 29, 1944, and awarded to any member, officer, or master of an American ship or any foreign ship operated for the US Maritime Commission or the War Shipping Administration, who is commended by the Administrator for meritorious conduct not of such a nature as to warrant the Distinguished Service Medal.

NASA EXCEPTIONAL
SCIENTIFIC ACHIEVEMENT
MEDAL

NASA PUBLIC SERVICE
MEDAL

NASA EXCEPTIONAL
SERVICE MEDAL

NASA EXCEPTIONAL
ENGINEERING
ACHIEVEMENT MEDAL

NASA SPACE FLIGHT MEDAL

MERCHANT MARINE
DISTINGUISHED SERVICE
MEDAL

THE MARINER'S MEDAL

Authorized by Congress on May 10, 1943, and awarded to any seaman who, while serving on a ship of the U.S. Merchant Marine, is wounded, undergoes physical injury, or suffers through dangerous exposure as a result of an act of the enemy of the United States. The Purple Heart Medal would have been awarded for similar service in the military.

GALLANT SHIP MEDALLION AND CITATION PLAQUE

This medallion and plaque was established on August 29, 1944. There were only nine awards of the Gallant Ship Medallion and Citation Plaque during World War II and only one awarded for the Korean War period. There have been thirty awards for the 1956–1984 period. Personnel serving on the cited ship are entitled to wear the Gallant Ship Citation Ribbon.

THE GALLANT SHIP CITATION RIBBON

Established on August 29, 1944, and awarded to officers and seamen serving aboard a ship that has been awarded the Gallant Ship Citation Plaque. This was designed by members of the US Maritime Administration, and shows a small silver sea horse worn in the center of the ribbon.

THE COMBAT BAR

Authorized on May 10, 1943, and awarded to members of the Merchant Marine who served on a ship when it was attacked or damaged by the enemy or an instrument of war, such as a mine. This distinctive award is a ribbon bar only.

The following awards are presented to officers and seamen for service aboard ships of the Merchant Marine in various theaters of war during World War II.

MERCHANT MARINE DEFENSE BAR

Authorized on August 24, 1944 and awarded to officers

and men serving aboard United States merchant ships between September 8, 1939 and December 7, 1941.

ATLANTIC WAR ZONE BAR

Authorized on May 10, 1943 and awarded to officers and men of ships operated for or by the War Shipping Administration for service in the Atlantic War Zone during World War II.

PACIFIC WAR ZONE BAR

Authorized on May 10, 1943, this was awarded to officers and men of ships operated by or for the War Shipping Administration for service in the Pacific War Zone.

MEDITERRANEAN-MIDDLE EAST WAR ZONE BAR

Authorized on May 10, 1943, and awarded to officers and men of ships operated by or for the War Shipping Administration for service in the named war zone.

MERCHANT MARINE VICTORY MEDAL

Authorized on August 8, 1946, and awarded to officers and men for service on any vessel operated by or for the US Maritime Commission or the War Shipping Administration for thirty days service between December 7, 1941 and September 3, 1945.

THE MERCHANT MARINE KOREAN SERVICE RIBBON

Created on July 24, 1956 by the US Maritime Administration. This was awarded to officers and men for service aboard merchant vessels flying the American flag in waters adjacent to Korea between June 30, 1950 and September 30, 1953, during the conflict in Korea.

MERCHANT MARINE MERITORIOUS SERVICE MEDAL

MERCHANT MARINE WORLD WAR TWO VICTORY MEDAL

MERCHANT MARINE VIETNAM SERVICE RIBBON

Authorized on May 20, 1968, and awarded to officers and men who served aboard merchant vessels flying the American flag in Vietnam waters at any time from July 4, 1965 to August 15, 1973.

MARINER'S MEDAL

CHAPTER FOURTEEN
RARE AND UNUSUAL MEDALS OF THE UNITED STATES

All of the following decorations were authorized by Acts of Congress. They were created to commemorate special acts and deeds. They were so rarely awarded that they are seldom found in even the most advanced collections.

THE BAILEY MEDAL

Authorized by the Navy Department on December 1, 1885, this medal was awarded annually to a naval apprentice with an outstanding record, in memory of Admiral Theodorus Bailey, (1805–1877). It is a small gold medal with a suspender resembling a block and tackle and a navy blue ribbon.

CARDENAS MEDAL OF HONOR

Authorized by Joint Resolution of Congress, May 3, 1900, the Cardenas medal was awarded to officers and men of the Revenue Cutter Service, (now the Coast Guard) *USRCS Hudson*, for gallantry on May 11, 1898 during the Spanish/American War. A large table-top medal and smaller medal in gold, silver and bronze were issued.

RELIEF OF THE WHALERS MEDAL

These medals were authorized by Congress on June 28, 1902, and awarded to the officers of the Revenue Cutter Service on the *USRCS Bear*. They made an overland expedition to relieve 300 men on eight whaling ships caught by Arctic ice in the vicinity of Point Barrow, Alaska.

THE CONQUEST OF YELLOW FEVER MEDAL

Authorized by Congress on February 28, 1929. This gold medal was awarded to Major Walter Reed and his staff and Army volunteers who waged the successful campaign against the dread yellow fever in 1900–1901, making it possible to build the Panama Canal.

THE PANAMA CANAL SERVICE MEDAL

Authorized in 1907 by President Theodore Roosevelt and presented by the President to any citizen of the United States who served the government satisfactorily on the Isthmus of Panama for two continuous years in the building of the Panama Canal.

THE SPECIALLY MERITORIOUS MEDAL
(NAVY AND MARINE CORPS)

Authorized by Congress on March 3, 1901, this medal is a bronze cross pattee created to recognize "officers and enlisted men of the US Navy and Marine Corps who rendered specially meritorious service, otherwise than in battle," during the war with Spain in 1898. There were only 93 recipients of this award.

Congress also authorized a series of medals for Life Saving acts that were performed by foreign nationals. They were usually awarded for the saving of American lives from the dangers of the sea and include such medals as the Presidential Life Saving Medals in Gold, Silver and Bronze.

THE NC-4 MEDAL

Authorized by Congress on February 9, 1929, and awarded to Navy Commander John H. Towers for "conceiving, organizing and commanding the first transatlantic flight" and to officers and crew members of Navy flying boat NC-4 who crossed the Atlantic with him in May of 1919.

THE TEXAS CAVALRY MEDAL

Authorized on April 16, 1924. The medal was awarded to officers and men of two brigades of the Texas National Guard Cavalry for service on the Mexican Border from September 25 to November 11, 1918.

AIR MAIL FLYER'S MEDAL OF HONOR

Established by an Act of Congress on February 14, 1931, which authorized the President of the United States to award a medal of honor to any person employed as a pilot in the Air Mail Service of the United States who distinguished himself by heroism or extraordinary achievement while carrying the mail.

AMERICAN TYPHUS COMMISSION MEDAL

Authorized by Executive Order on December 24, 1942, a personal decoration awarded by the President to members of the commission for meritorious service in connection with the work of the Typhus Control Commission.

■ CIVILIAN DECORATIONS ■ AND AWARDS

Many people who were not in military uniform served with great distinction during World War II. In recognition of this a series of decorations and awards were created expressly for presentation to civilians.

THE MEDAL OF MERIT

Authorized on July 20, 1942, and awarded by the President of the United States to US civilians and civilians of friendly foreign nations waging war under a joint declaration with the United States who distinguish themselves by the performance of outstanding services. The Medal of Merit is the civilian Legion of Merit.

THE PRESIDENTIAL MEDAL OF FREEDOM

Founded by President Truman in 1945 to reward meritorious, war-connected acts and services. Awarded only nine times by President Truman and thirteen times by President Eisenhower, the medal shown is the first style badge, which came in only one class. This medal was redesigned and reestablished by President Kennedy in three classes.

BAILEY MEDAL

CARDENAS MEDAL OF HONOR,
Cased Set

THE CONQUEST OF YELLOW FEVER MEDAL

THE SPECIALLY MERITORIOUS MEDAL,
(1898)

TEXAS CAVALRY MEDAL

MEDAL OF MERIT

NC-4 MEDAL,
Obverse

**PRESIDENTIAL MEDAL
OF FREEDOM**

DEPARTMENT OF DEFENSE
DISTINGUISHED CIVILIAN SERVICE MEDAL

Established on November 26, 1954, and awarded to civilian employees of the Defense Department for exceptional devotion to duty and for contributions to the operation of the Department.

It is the highest award given by the Secretary of Defense to civilian employees.

DEPARTMENT OF DEFENSE
DISTINGUISHED PUBLIC SERVICE MEDAL

Presented to civilians who do not derive their principal livelihood from government employment, but who have rendered distinguished public service to the Department of Defense and/or one of its components.

SECRETARY OF DEFENSE
OUTSTANDING PUBLIC SERVICE MEDAL

A junior award to the previous medal, it has the same design, but is in silver. It is awarded by the Secretary to civilians not employed by the Federal government who render outstanding public service to the Department of Defense.

SECRETARY OF DEFENSE
MERITORIOUS CIVILIAN SERVICE MEDAL

Authorized on March 4, 1955, and awarded by the Secretary of Defense to civilian employees of the government in recognition of exceptionally meritorious service to the Department.

ARMY DISTINGUISHED CIVILIAN
SERVICE MEDAL

Authorized on September 17, 1956, and awarded by the Secretary of the Army to private citizens, government officials and technical personnel who serve the Army as advisors or consultants, and who have rendered distinguished service or made substantial contributions to the Army's mission.

ARMY OUTSTANDING CIVILIAN
SERVICE MEDAL

Awarded by the Secretary of the Army as a junior award, the services must be the same as required for the Distinguished Civilian Service Medal but to a lesser degree.

ARMY EXCEPTIONAL CIVILIAN SERVICE MEDAL

Authorized in 1960, and awarded to United States Army civilian employees who have rendered exceptional services to the Department of the Army. It can also be awarded for an act of heroism, involving risk of life, in direct benefit to the government and its personnel. If awarded for heroism, the word "Bravery" appears on the reverse of the medal.

ARMY MERITORIOUS CIVILIAN SERVICE MEDAL

Authorized by the Secretary of the Army in 1960 as an award to private citizens, federal officials and technical personnel including consultants, who render outstanding services to major commands, but not to a degree high enough to merit the Exceptional Civilian Service Medal.

NAVY DISTINGUISHED CIVILIAN SERVICE MEDAL

This is the highest honorary award conferred by the Secretary of the Navy to civilian employees of the Department of the Navy. It is awarded for extraordinary contributions that deserve the highest recognition. It can also be awarded for great courage in the face of danger that results in direct benefit to the government or its personnel.

NAVY SUPERIOR CIVILIAN SERVICE MEDAL

Awarded by the Secretary of the Navy for superior civilian service or contributions which have resulted in exceptional benefit to the Navy. The services are of a lesser degree than that required for the Distinguished Civilian Service Medal.

NAVY DISTINGUISHED PUBLIC SERVICE MEDAL

Established in July, 1951, the medal is awarded to US citizens not employed by the Navy for heroic acts and significant contributions which help accomplish the Navy's mission. This medal has very rarely been awarded.

MEDAL OF FREEDOM

DEPARTMENT OF DEFENSE DISTINGUISHED CIVILIAN SERVICE

DEPARTMENT OF DEFENSE DISTINGUISHED PUBLIC SERVICE MEDAL

SECRETARY OF DEFENSE OUTSTANDING PUBLIC SERVICE

ARMY MERITORIOUS CIVILIAN SERVICE MEDAL

NAVY SUPERIOR CIVILIAN SERVICE MEDAL

AIR FORCE CIVILIAN MEDAL FOR VALOR

SECRETARY OF DEFENSE MERITORIOUS CIVILIAN SERVICE

CAPTAIN ROBERT DEXTER CONRAD MEDAL

Established in December 1956, this medal is awarded by the Secretary of the Navy for Distinguished scientific achievement to the Navy. This unusual medal is awarded once a year and is named in honor of Captain Robert Dexter Conrad, US Navy, the architect of the Navy scientific research program.

US NAVY DISTINGUISHED ACHIEVEMENT IN SCIENCE AWARD

Authorized in January, 1961, this rarely-seen award is given to reward major breakthroughs in science of value to the United States Navy.

AIR FORCE CIVILIAN MEDAL FOR VALOR

Established in 1965, and awarded by the Secretary of the Air Force to civilians serving in any capacity with the US Air Force, who demonstrate unusual competence or courage while on duty.

AIR FORCE COMMAND CIVILIAN MEDAL FOR VALOR

Established in 1965, it is a junior award in silver, awarded to civilians who demonstrate unusual courage.

AIR FORCE EXCEPTIONAL CIVILIAN SERVICE MEDAL

Established on August 30, 1948, this medal is awarded to civilian employees of the Department of the Air Force for exceptional service rendered to the US Air Force. This award may also be presented for an act of heroism involving voluntary risk of life.

AIR FORCE MERITORIOUS CIVILIAN SERVICE MEDAL

Originally a lapel pin and certificate, it evolved into its present form as a junior decoration to the Exceptional Civilian Service medal in 1967. This award is comparable to the Meritorious Service Medal for military personnel.

COAST GUARD DISTINGUISHED PUBLIC SERVICE AWARD

Established in 1984, this medal is awarded to any person, who is not employed by the Coast Guard, who renders one of the following services: extraordinary heroism in advancing the Coast Guard's mission; a personal and direct contribution to the Coast Guard that produced tangible results that measurably improved or expedited their mission; exceptional cooperation in public or international affairs.

COAST GUARD MERITORIOUS PUBLIC SERVICE AWARD

This award was established at the same time as the previous award, and the requirements are for similar services but of a lesser degree than that required for the higher decoration.

DEPARTMENT OF THE ARMY COMMANDER'S AWARD FOR CIVILIAN SERVICE

One of the newer junior awards of the Department of the Army which allows commanders of small Army units to recognize civilians who have assisted them in the performance of their duties and advanced the goals of the US Army.

AIR FORCE COMMAND CIVILIAN MEDAL FOR VALOR

AIR FORCE EXCEPTIONAL CIVILIAN SERVICE MEDAL

AIR FORCE MERITORIOUS CIVILIAN SERVICE MEDAL

COAST GUARD DISTINGUISHED PUBLIC SERVICE AWARD

UNITED NATIONS SERVICE MEDAL

REPUBLIC OF VIETNAM GALLANTRY CROSS

REPUBLIC OF VIETNAM SERVICE MEDAL

MULTINATIONAL FORCE AND OBSERVERS MEDAL

■ AWARDS OF FOREIGN ■ GOVERNMENTS TO US MILITARY PERSONNEL

It is the policy of the Department of Defense, conforming to the consent of Congress, that awards from foreign governments to members of the United States military may be accepted only in recognition of active combat service or for outstanding or unusually meritorious performance.

THE PHILIPPINE DEFENSE RIBBON

Authorized in 1944 and awarded for United States Armed Forces personnel for service in the defense of the Philippines from December 8, 1941 to June 15, 1942.

THE PHILIPPINE LIBERATION RIBBON

Authorized in 1944, it is awarded to personnel of the United States Armed Forces for participation in the liberation of the Philippines from October 17, 1944 to September 3, 1945.

PHILIPPINE INDEPENDENCE RIBBON

Authorized by the Philippine Commonwealth Government, Army Headquarters in 1946. Awarded to personnel of the United States Armed Forces who are recipients of the Philippine Defense Ribbon or the Philippine Liberation Ribbon.

PHILIPPINE PRESIDENTIAL UNIT CITATION

Authorized in 1946, this award is made in the name of the President of the Republic of the Philippines to outstanding units cited for gallantry in action during the war.

■ KOREAN WAR PERIOD, ■ JUNE 27, 1950 to JULY 27, 1955

REPUBLIC OF KOREA PRESIDENTIAL UNIT CITATION

This unit award was presented to members of the United Nations Command for outstanding service in Korea, under the same conditions as Presidential Unit Citation.

UNITED NATIONS SERVICE MEDAL

Authorized by the United Nations General Assembly on December 12, 1950, and authorized for United States Armed Forces personnel on November 27, 1951, and awarded to members of the armed forces who participated in United Nations actions in Korea between June 27, 1950 and July 27, 1954.

UNITED NATIONS MEDAL

Authorized by the United Nations on July 30, 1959, and approved by U.N. Executive Order on January 7, 1964, this is awarded to service members who have served in the United Nations for a period of six months with one of the following: United Nations Observation Group in Lebanon (UNOGIL), United Nations Truce Supervisory Group in Palestine (UNTSO), UN Military Observer Group in India and Pakistan (UNMOGIP), United Nations Security Forces, Hollandia (UNSFH).

■ THE VIETNAM CONFLICT ■ March 1, 1961–March 28, 1974

REPUBLIC OF VIETNAM PRESIDENTIAL UNIT CITATION

Originally created as the Vietnam Friendship Ribbon, it was recreated as the Presidential Unit Citation in 1961, and awarded to cited units under the same conditions required for the award of the Presidential Unit Citation of the United States.

REPUBLIC OF VIETNAM GALLANTRY CROSS

Established on August 15, 1950 as an award for outstanding bravery by officers and enlisted men who distinguish themselves conspicuously by gallantry in action at the risk of life. It corresponds to the French Croix de Guerre.

REPUBLIC OF VIETNAM UNIT GALLANTRY CITATION

Awarded to members of the United States Armed Forces for valorous achievement in combat during the Vietnam conflict, March 1, 1961 through March 28, 1974.

REPUBLIC OF VIETNAM CIVIL ACTIONS UNIT CITATION

Awarded by the Republic of Vietnam to units of the United States Armed Forces in recognition of meritorious civil action service. It is also awarded to other friendly nations serving in Vietnam during the Vietnam conflict.

REPUBLIC OF VIETNAM SERVICE MEDAL

Awarded to members of the Armed Forces who have served for a six-month period in Vietnam, its surrounding waters or in air support against an armed enemy in Vietnam between March 1, 1961 and March 28, 1973. The time limit is waived if the recipient was killed, wounded or captured at any time before the limit.

MULTINATIONAL FORCE AND OBSERVERS MEDAL

Approval to accept and wear this medal was granted by the Department of Defense on July 26, 1984. It is awarded to members of the United States Armed Forces who after August 3, 1981, have served with the Multinational force and Observes for at least 90 days. The force, (MFO) was created to act as a buffer between Israel and Egypt in the Sinai Peninsula.

▮ BIBLIOGRAPHY ▮

The following books have been invaluable in the preparation of this work:

Shoulder Patch Insignia of the United States Armed Forces Wolf Appleton. New York.

US Military Shoulder Patches of the United States Armed Forces 4th Edition. Jack Britton and George Washington Jr. Tulsa Oklahoma.

Air Force Collecting Cliff Gates. M.C.N. Press, Tulsa, Okalhoma.

Elite Unit Insignia of the Vietnam War Leroy Thomson. Arms and Armour Press, London, UK.

US Army Cloth Insignia 1941 to the Present Brian L. Davis. Arms and Armour Press, London, UK.

Army Badges and Insignia of World War 2 Guido Rosignolli. Blandford, UK.

Army Badges and Insignia Since 1945 Guido Rosignolli. Blandford, UK.